GW00363804

Introduction to ANTIQUES

Introduction to ANTIQUES

Therle Hughes

Country Life Books

title page illustration
Silver mustard pot by C. R. Ashbee. 1903.

Introduction to Antiques has been developed from material originally published by *Homes and Gardens* in 1971. The Publishers wish to express their thanks to the Editor of that journal.

Distributed for Country Life Books by
The Hamlyn Publishing Group Limited
London . New York . Sydney . Toronto
Astronaut House, Feltham, Middlesex, England

First published 1977

ISBN 0 600 30346 2

Printed in England by
Cox & Wyman Limited

Contents

Introduction

Lovely materials, skilled craftsmanship, graceful function-filling design – these surely make our antiques treasurable. This brief book is for beginners and can merely outline the background story, offering pointers towards understanding and enjoyment. It suggests ways to identify the items that particularly pleased men and women down the centuries, the styles they favoured and the techniques that were developed to meet their needs.

My hope is that would-be collectors will be stirred to adventure further – that they may trace chronologically the development of furniture locks and handles, say, or the changing shapes of teapots or decanters, and find the pattern of contrasting fashions implied by such terms as Rococo, Gothic, Neo-classical, Arts and Crafts and Art Nouveau. Especially I hope they may visit museums, shops and stately homes, gazing long and hard at authentic pieces. It is better still if they can handle them too, until it becomes possible to sense instinctively their period and status, even to feel welcomed into that past world by those who once used them.

The complexities and confusions involved in collecting antiques make successes all the sweeter. Always of course it is important to remember that every triumph prompted imitations. Some of today's most prized items were introduced as cost-cutting substitutes, such as blue-painted delftware, for example, and enamelled white glass. Reproductions were adored by status-conscious Victorians and continue to this day: shame attaches only to the deliberate price-inflated fake.

In each chapter I have outlined the story period by period and suggested items typical of their day and popular with collectors, but the range is endless. Small pots and boxes, for example, could be mentioned time and again through every chapter and frequently in my final miscellanea. Today many collectors are finding a seeming remoteness and great charm even among items less than one hundred years old. Here especially experience must guide their choice, for a background knowledge of the finest traditional work can best aid in assessing these antiques of tomorrow.

If, as I hope, this book prompts the beginner to delve more deeply into some of the subjects, I suggest enquiry at a local library. It would be impossible here to given an adequate list of suitable books.

Early 19th-century figure group in brittle earthenware.

Furniture

Seldom can anyone put an exact date upon an antique furnishing. Indeed if a date has been carved upon it, the item is immediately suspect. Yet even beginner-collectors find, surprisingly quickly, that small details are deciding for them almost subconsciously whether a period piece is 'right'. And what a joy that is.

Among furniture, fashions changed slowly, of course, and overlapped. The work was strong and made to last, and those who commissioned it from joiner and cabinetmaker tended to keep to safe familiar patterns. At the same time lavish notions for stately homes might be drastically modified to meet the needs of yeoman home-making.

Even as late as Victorian days traditional fine craftsmanship challenged the new marvels of the machine processes and mass production responsible for much ill-designed, shoddy work. And Edwardians could already witness a little of the modern movement's functional grace.

How it all began

Some grand furniture remains to us from Tudor days–straight-backed panelled armchairs, extending 'draw' tables, carved and panelled bedsteads. Medieval carpenters had knocked up chests and benches of hammered planks, but Tudor joiners perfected the all-important mortise-and-tenon joints characteristic of this period's 'joined' and panelled furniture, witnessed by the slightly projecting heads of the wooden dowel pins that secured them. At this time, too, the turner added massive ornamental swellings to his lathe-shaped bedposts and table legs; often these swellings were further enriched with carvings such as cup-and-cover designs. The period's carving was bold and heavy in contrast to simple geometrical patterns in flat-surfaced inlays of contrasting woods. Much early furniture was painted, and great use was made of elegant iron handles and hinges.

This splendid Tudor exuberance was followed by the extraordinary contrasts of the 17th century. Wealthy early Stuart families enjoyed new chances of privacy such as parlour-dining with smaller single (armless) chairs set around folding gate-leg tables. Even hugger-mugger storage in deep chests was im-

Mid 17th-century oak chest showing deep mouldings with conspicuous corner mitres as decorative detail. The small panel inlays are of silver, glass and fabric. Text page 10. Victoria and Albert Museum, London.

proved by including drawers in the mule-chest, transitional between lidded chest and chest of drawers. Carved ornament might be reduced to shallow repetition of lunette or guilloche pattern. But pride in good workmanship was expressed in carefully mitred, deeply moulded panels and orderly turned ornament such as ball-and-reel outlines to chair and table legs, left square, of course, for all joints. Seats might be covered in leather or the woollen pile known as turkey work.

1660s–1700s: the rise of the cabinetmaker

In contrast, Charles II and his court in 1660 returned from exile on the Continent requiring the ornate furniture of the cabinetmaker. This was a turning point indeed. For the first time construction was masked by a smooth glued-on surface of veneer. This thin veneer wood could be chosen for beauty regardless of strength, walnut being most popular, including knotty burrwood. Sometimes the veneer was applied in symmetrical patterns of contrasting grains (parquetry). More elaborately, fragments of veneer in contrasting colours were fitted together to make patterns (marquetry) of flowers and birds or the later intricate leafy scrolling and 'seaweed'.

Chests of drawers and bureaux became fashionable, showing a new delicacy in such detail as the dovetails joining the fronts and sides of drawers and the earliest brass drop handles. The early tall cabinet-on-stand was rectangular with characteristic straight cornice and swelling frieze above cabinet doors or a fall-front that opened forward and downward from the top to reveal a dozen small drawers, perhaps, around a central cupboard.

Other specialist craftsmen set up as carvers and gilders making ornate furniture such as stands for luxury cabinets of Oriental lacquer. Some gilded and silvered wooden furniture was patterned in low relief on all visible surfaces with gesso, a plaster and size composition, for such new pleasures as wall mirrors and delicate-legged side tables.

Even the humble turner had to extend his skill, and a charac-

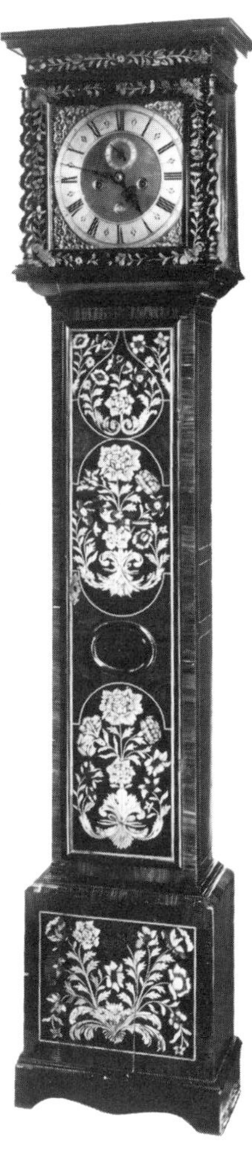

Intricate marquetry on a splendid early long case clock. The clock mechanism made by John Pitcher of London, about 1695. The hood is flanked by swash-turned or 'barley sugar' twist turning. Text opposite page.

teristic of late Stuart chairs and small tables is the swash-turned or barley sugar twist. This is often a conspicuous detail of the late 17th-century armchair which has a tall back and outward curving arms. New features here include comfortable panels of caning in the seat and in the framework of the backward-sloping back. Carving of the broad back cresting is often a pattern of leafy scrolls, perhaps surrounding 'boys' supporting a crown, and this is repeated in another new feature, a broad ornamental stretcher set high between the front legs.

In the last decade of the century many 'William and Mary' chairs were dominated by deep S-scrolls. These crested the tall back, supported the sagging arms and served as massive front legs.

1700s–1720s: Queen Anne grace

Queen Anne reigned only from 1702 to 1714, but the style associated with her name continued into George I's reign. The period is associated especially with a new demand for occasional furniture–fashionably walnut still in solid and veneer–and a new care for its convenience and graceful detail. The period's appealing love of curves runs right through its furniture, from the arching tops of mirror and cabinet through the comfortable shoulder-fitting walnut chair-back to the bold rounded knee and incurving taper of the cabriole leg. This leg design is especially interesting as it quickly escaped the restrictions of horizontal stretchers save in such new upholstered luxuries as the winged armchair and early settee.

Fashionable beds were immensely tall, but other bedroom furniture looks delightful in any room today, such as the dressing table with an arched kneehole flanked by small drawers. The swinging dressing glass with supports mounted on a small stand of tiny fitted compartments would have been flanked originally by matching candlestands. Occasional tables were made specifically for card playing and for writing. These, too, lost the ornate turned legs and elaborately curved stretchers of the 17th century's end in favour of free-standing cabrioles. An early scroll-footed pole screen would be an obvious accompaniment. Delight in Oriental lacquer continued with English imitations known as japanning that looked particularly splendid on longcase (grandfather) clocks.

1720s–1750: early Georgian vigour

Escallop shell carving on walnut, trademark as it were of the previous period, continued into early Georgian days (purely for convenience dated 1720–50). But the up-and-coming wood was mahogany, dark and heavy and so dense that it was the pride and despair of carvers. Detail such as ball-and-claw feet and eagle-head chair arm terminals, laboriously carved in this early 'Spanish' or 'San Domingo' mahogany, have retained an almost metallic vigour and crispness. The huge tree girth meant that, for example, each flap of a large folding table could be cut from a single plank supported by a single hinged leg. This gate table was free of the stretchers and extra legs that cluttered the older gate-leg table.

At the same time a new delicacy could be introduced in enduring pierced work. As always, chairs are an interesting indication of fashion. Here the change was away from a roundly arched back supporting a central splat in simple baluster outline. Instead early Georgian mahogany suited designs with a cupid's bow cresting rail making a sharp angle with its side supports and enclosing a boldly pierced and carved splat.

William Kent, 1686–1748, and his followers designed massive furniture in the manner of their classical 'Palladian' architecture such as heavy console tables bracketed to the wall dado. But the period is remembered for such unpretentious pleasures as the corner chair for card players and the reading chair for the horseman to straddle, leaning his arms on its widened cresting rail and displaying his silken coat tails.

Around 1750–1760: mid Georgian gaiety

It is still possible to find a mansion with state rooms furnished in the full magnificence of the mid 18th-century's wonderful pierced and carved mahogany. Items may range from tables and chairs to the elegant little three-legged wash basin stand for the hair powdering closet, now sometimes misnamed a wig stand.

Brightly gilded mounts set off the mahogany, then including Cuban wood in richly grained veneers. But for a touch of fantasy cabinetmakers might introduce Oriental lacquer and imitation European japanning on such handsome furnishings as the low set of drawers, often enclosed by wide cupboard doors, then known as a commode. Cabinets were fashionable too, glazed

Tall bureau of the early 18th century decorated with figures, flowers and landscape scenes in the Chinese taste in gold and colours on a brilliant vermilion ground. Text page 13.

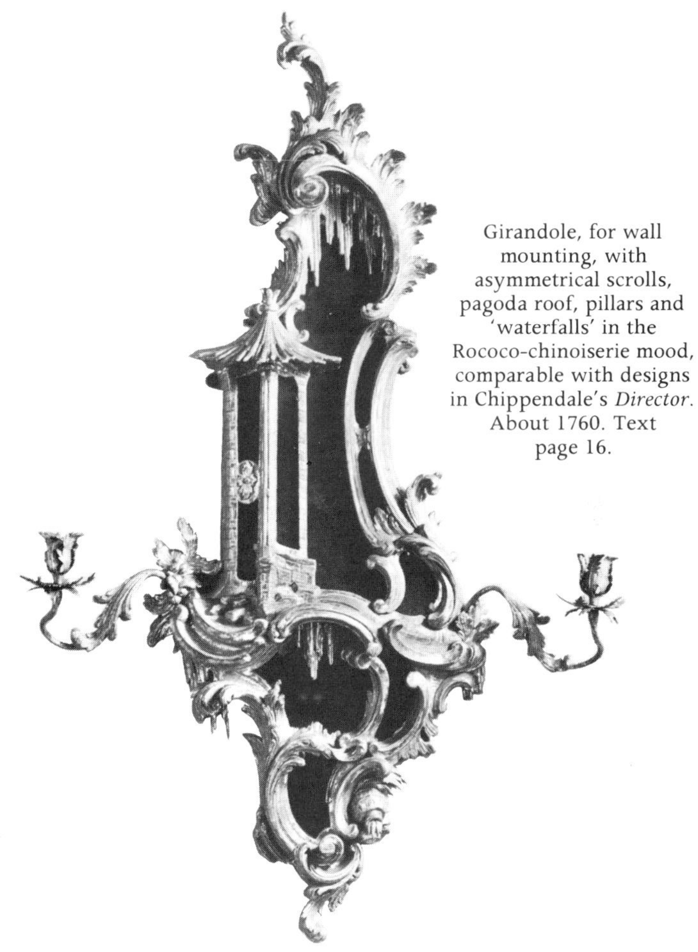

Girandole, for wall mounting, with asymmetrical scrolls, pagoda roof, pillars and 'waterfalls' in the Rococo-chinoiserie mood, comparable with designs in Chippendale's *Director*. About 1760. Text page 16.

with the period's improved crown glass held by the strong but slender glazing bars made practicable by using dense mahogany.

Furniture made at this period is often dubbed Chippendale because Thomas Chippendale brought out the first edition of his important *Gentleman and Cabinet Maker's Director* in 1754. This offered the furniture trade a wide range of designs. Reproductions of these may be by contemporaries or later copyists (including Victorians), but known work by the Chippendale firm followed later 18th-century fashions. For minor rooms this period indulged in uninhibited romantic gaiety, its asymmetrical scrolling ornament carved with all manner of fantastic incident from pillars and waterfalls to Chinamen and their pagodas.

This passing pleasure in imagined 'Chinese' and 'Gothic' ornament was a recurrent phase of home adornment. Around the mid 18th century it prompted some unusual furniture including chairs–the 'Chinese' with lattice backs and straight, pierced legs, and the 'Gothic' with church window shaping and cluster-column legs. Chippendale's lesser rivals included Ince and Mayhew who published their *Universal System of Household Furniture*, 1759–62.

Pillar-and-claw furniture was never better, with three crisply curved cabriole legs supporting a turned and carved pillar and an adjustable firescreen, perhaps, or a circular table top. The most familiar–and reproduced–circular table has its rim carved in a series of cyma curves and sharp angles known as a piecrust. Brass bail handles for drawers appeared in a stronger design, with boldly pierced backplates. A finely curved, superbly veneered drawer might have a separate relief-ornamented plate for each end of the swinging handle.

1760s–1780s: the mellow mood of Neo-classicism

Architect Robert Adam, 1728–92, designed many furnishings to suit his mansions, and his admiration for the classical world led to the Neo-classical vogue. Furniture was designed for contemporary requirements but with deference to classical ideals, in attractively proportioned geometrical shapes with ornament flat or in low relief. Everything had to be cleanly symmetrical: the favourite outline was the bland oval medallion or the pointed-end, shuttle-shaped ellipse, for panels, mirror frames, chair-backs, even the machine-stamped brass backplates of drawer handles.

Enrichment was confined to detail taken from classical ornament. This included urns, swags of drapery, pendulous bell-flowers, saucer-like circular paterae, the anthemion or stylised honeysuckle flower, and much vertical convex fluting known as reeding which suited the period's tapering straight legs.

Neo-classical Adam mood expressed in mahogany chair with lyre back (with gilded strings) and tapering wave-moulded legs. Text below.

All this is found in mahogany ranging from the magnificent flame-grained Cuban variety to the cheaper Honduras (baywood) in solid and veneer. Even country work in oak and native fruitwoods might be banded with mahogany to add an uneasy touch of fashion. Mahogany contrasted splendidly with gilded furnishings such as hanging mirror frames of wood and composition and the familiar lyre-back chair, but Adam's somewhat effeminate designs especially suited the pale golden colour and marvellous silky grain of satinwood. This might be banded with exotic kingwood or tulipwood, but in the 1770s such extravagance—on a drawing room commode, perhaps—called for Neo-classical figures painted in the style of Angelica Kauffmann or medallions composed in delicately coloured marquetry. Back-ground veneer might be of the grey-green dyed sycamore known as harewood. Cheaper substitutes included wood painted all over in a pale shade. Wedgwood's classical figure plaques in subdued matt-surfaced jasperware were mounted on cabinet furniture of the 1780s.

Another 'name' important to this period is George Hepple-white. Nothing is known of his own work, but his *Cabinet Maker and Upholsterer's Guide* was first published in 1788, two years after his death. This shows a charming homely interpre-tation of Neo-classicism with a simple flowing serpentine grace, from gently undulating pediment to smoothly out-curving 'French' feet. A contemporary, Thomas Shearer, is associated with designs in the anonymous and often re-issued *Cabinet Maker's London Book Of Prices*, another influential trade manual. For example, Shearer in 1788 first illustrated the period's de-lightful fitted sideboard. Much elegant cabinet furniture was made by such large-scale London manufacturers as George Seddon, 1727–1801, and his sons. The important furniture-maker Robert Gillow of Lancaster established a London branch in about 1760, and the firm has left marked furniture and design records dating to the end of the period reviewed in this book.

Collectable dining room items include brass-banded ma-hogany plate pails and wine cisterns and the useful butler's tray on its folding stand. But the choice is endless, including the pleasant little pembroke table with folding flaps resting on fly brackets. Hanging corner cupboards are delightfully unpre-tentious, as is the 'chest of drawers' for the guest-visited dressing room that opens to reveal a fitted dressing table or secretary drawer.

Victorians shared our pleasure in 'Hepplewhite' chairs but might distort the proportions of those shield-shaped backs and tapering wave-moulded legs.

1790s–1800s: the Sheraton view of furnishing

Poor Thomas Sheraton, 1751–1806, died in poverty but now is renowned for the style of furniture recorded in his pattern books, especially in his *Cabinet Maker and Upholsterer's Drawing Book*, published 1791–94. In many ways his designs for light cabinet work and squarer chairs show a transition between the sweeping curves and serpentine shaping of waning Neo-classical grace and the heavy square solidity of the Regency's Greco-Roman-Etruscan styles. No work by him is known, but his designs often have a personal, womanly charm about them. He accepted the period's drastic economies with recourse to

Carlton House writing table in finely grained golden satinwood. Typical features are the D-shaped back topped with a pierced brass gallery, square handles and tassel-top legs. Text page 20.

poorer qualities of wood and more cheaply painted ornament. But his designs are often full of ingenuity at a time when men and women had a liking for contrivances such as moveable desk fitments, elaborate pouched worktables, adjustable mirrors and firescreens. His Carlton House writing table design has never gone out of production.

Another late 18th-century form of desk, known as a tambour or reed top, had a flexible rounded lid composed of narrow laths glued horizontally on stiff fabric, its ends sliding in grooved runners. A sideboard might have a central tambour cupboard door to slide out of sight in the same manner. Sheraton shared his period's pleasure in neat little feet to much light, delicate furniture such as thimble toes on tapering turned legs and great

Windsor armchair of the late 18th century but retaining the cabriole leg outline, here linked by 'cow horn' stretchers. Text opposite page. Victoria and Albert Museum, London.

use of brass casters. The claw legs tend to be very slender in a sagging outline on such pillar-and-claw furniture as the tiers of diminishing trays known as dumb waiters and the individual tables for tea guests then known as teapoys.

The period's plainer squarer outlines are seen in square-ended, bow-fronted chests of drawers and drawing room commodes. A chair might be cane-seated again, the back supports topped with an ornamental panel above a central pattern of cross-bars. The set of the arms contributed to the high-shouldered effect.

Many comfortable windsor chairs date to this period even when their legs retain the old cabriole outline. These splendid country chairs were made to stand endless rough handling on flagstone floors. The saddle-shaped seat was thick enough to be drilled with holes for the springy hooped back and the out-jutting legs, and was comfortable even without a cushion – very different from the smooth polished seat of the hall chair or settee offering minimal comfort to the waiting messenger.

1800 – 1820s: the Regency style

A scroll-ended sofa, a long narrow sofa-table with folding flaps at the ends instead of the sides, a jaunty little chair with scimitar legs rounding out back and front in simple concave curves from seat to floor – we all know some of the characteristics of down-to-earth Regency furnishings, far too abundant still to have been restricted to the actual Regency years, 1811 – 20. The style had its beginnings in the 1790s when a deeper archaeological interest in the classical world prompted actual imitation of ancient couches, chairs and the like rather than the 18th century's Neo-classical invention and superficial ornament. Added to all this, Napoleon's campaigns, and the 1802 peace, prompted enthusiasm for sheathed caryatid figures, winged lions, lotus buds and other striking Egyptian detail.

This period has left many especially collectable pieces in the trestle style (horse was the term at the time) such as long dressing glasses, games tables with reversible tops and pouch worktables. Other attractive Regency items include canterbury sheet music stands, banner firescreens, the small square desk with drawers down the side known as a davenport and the tea caddy mounted on a stand which this period knew as a teapoy.

Fashionable brass ornament included increasingly ornate inlays, galleries, grills, feet (often with casters), including the ubiquitous lion mask with a ring in its mouth. Glass knob handles were soon followed by attractive flat wooden ones in the 1820s and some of painted china.

The late Georgian 1820s–1830s

Late Georgian is a period vaguely squeezed in between Regency and Victoriana and sometimes known by the German term 'Biedermeier'. Under George IV and William IV Regency fashions tended to become clumsy and florid while attempting early 18th-century French gaiety. Typical is the broad 'Greek' front leg spoiling the proportions of a low swept-back Regency chair. The massive swelling at knee height tapered quickly to a small foot, the width emphasised by vertical reeding or a cable twist.

Also unwelcome, perhaps, was the increasing use of French polishing to give wood surfaces a highly vulnerable gloss. But this period saw the introduction of easy-to-live-with balloon-back chairs as well as extremely cheap hardwearing mass-produced kitchen chairs (white Wycombes). Its contrasts include massive 'Gothic' solemnity and the scrolling gaiety of ornaments moulded in papier mâché.

1837–c. 1855: early Victoriana

Papier mâché furniture is a particularly endearing minor detail of the crowded early Victorian scene and eagerly collected today. Firescreens, small tables, teapoys, workboxes and most especially trays are to be found in varying qualities of this ware, its gleaming varnished ornament fixed by slow stoving and long hand polishing. Its restless curving shapes were acclaimed as revived Rococo or 'Louis XV', its gay all-over patterns including shimmering mother-of-pearl.

This, however, was only one feminine phase of a period that took itself very seriously. Another was romantic Gothic, with beds, chairs, even the popular nesting tables adorned with 'church window' architectural features. Designer A. W. N. Pugin really tried to incorporate Gothic design, but this heavy romantic escapism is most attractive perhaps as individualistic touches in arching cabinet door or galleried writing table.

This clinging to the safety of earlier styles is seen again in somewhat ungainly suites of furniture that Victorians dubbed Elizabethan although their characteristics such as twist turning had been introduced a century later. These may still confuse beginner-collectors until they recognise the proportions of much early Victorian furniture – long backed and short legged – taken to extremes in their favourite prie-dieu chair. This particular chair was especially approved as a way of showing off the home embroiderer's cross-stitch in Berlin wools. Such simple but laborious embroidery was popular from the 1830s as a part of the period's story-telling pictures and naturalistic flower ornament, recorded, too, in many a firescreen and footstool. Crude aniline textile dyes came only in the 1850s.

In its padded upholstery the chair expressed the period's very human pleasure in comfort, a reassurance sought, too, in plump fabric-smothered circular ottoman and two-person sociable sofa. Coiled springs for upholstered seating were patented as late as 1828 and only gradually supplemented long-proven curled horsehair and webbing.

Ever increasing numbers of middle class homes made huge demands on furniture craftsmen of all grades, and collectors can only be thankful that much shoddy cheap work has disintegrated and that more remains with beautifully fitting drawers and doors, fine dovetailed joints, well turned wooden knobs from a period that still chose magnificent rosewood for the drawing room and mahogany for dining.

1850s – 1870s: the assertive mid Victorians

Walnut, today regarded as the most Victorian of woods, was

largely a mid Victorian drawing room taste, with oak then for dining. But this was a period of assertive, substantial furniture in a confusion of period styles, which by the 1870s was dominated by the heavy rectilinear 'Louis XVI' outlines of late 18th-century French furnishings. Through the rest of the century there was much careful copying of 'Adam', 'Hepplewhite' and 'Sheraton' design.

Furniture was built to last and long treasured by well trained housemaids for its abundance of surface ornament such as ormolu and china plaques. Marquetry patterns are found in wood and in the brass-and-tortoiseshell ornament imitated in England from an old French process and known as boulle or buhl. Even photographs were mounted on furniture. The form

Satinwood cabinet by Wright and Mansfield, ornamented with marquetry, gilded mouldings and Wedgwood plaques. 1867. Text above. Victoria and Albert Museum, London.

of marquetry known as Tunbridge ware was popular in mosaic patterns. The tiny squares of differently coloured woods were fitted together in quantity to form geometrical patterns and pictorial scenes comparable with embroidered ornament in Berlin wool.

Mid Victorian exhibitions displayed huge furniture of ostentatious elaboration. Its superb craftsmanship defied such cheap imitation as the popular painted wood graining and shallow machine-cut carving. But it fostered reaction towards straightforward simplicity. This was expressed, for example, by reformist William Morris's associates from the 1860s with such enduring favourites as the familiar rush-seated chairs and settees inspired by Sussex country designs.

Minor pieces most likely to appeal to today's collectors range from the tiers of small shelves supported by delicately turned spindles in the corner whatnot to iron conservatory seats and tables. Another style that became popular in the 1860s was plain bentwood furniture such as round-backed chairs with caned seats and slender out-curving legs.

1880s–1900: late Victorian contradictions

Collectors who dismiss the late Victorian era for much shoddy, ill-designed furniture should realise that even at the time many important artists and designers, such as C. L. Eastlake and B. J. Talbert, were attempting to counteract pompous commercialism. Reformist professional designers and many enthusiastic amateurs sought a return to medieval ideas of straightforward craftsmanship enriched with imaginative ornament. The phrase Arts and Crafts covers a wide range of effort towards 'making useful things, making them well and making them beautiful', as declared by an important contributor, the architect-designer C. R. Ashbee.

This craft guild movement became active throughout the country, but for a far wider public the period offered much massive yet finicky furniture such as ebonised cabinets with marquetry grotesques between expanses of bevelled mirror glass surrounded by cupboards and shelves edged with tiny spindles. This was the era of the built-in 'cosy-corner' composed of padded seating and shelves for books and ornaments. Clean brass bedsteads were widely welcomed, but much bedroom furniture was heavy and space-wasting with deep pediments, pedestals and projecting corners.

The 1880s saw a vogue for minor furniture with a 'Moorish' glint of inlaid mother-of-pearl. But the main exotic influence came in the sensitive, delicate arts of newly 'discovered' Japan. Oriental textiles were imported by such firms as Liberty's and prompted, among other details, much use of bamboo. Under Japanese influence E. W. Godwin and others designed many light and elegant furnishings. But many more curiously shaped and fretted pieces of display furniture were listed as Anglo-Japanese in furniture trade catalogues that reflected current demand for novelty with such terms as aesthetic and quaint.

Turn of the century

Heavy, dark 'Jacobean' furniture was remarkably favoured around the turn of the century. Less tradition-bound alternatives included bright glossy satinwood and ebonised wood flatly inlaid. Architect-designer C. F. A. Voysey had an important influence in giving much simple oak and ebonised wood furniture the period look we associate especially with the early Edwardians, his chairs and case furniture having excessively tall, narrow uprights topped by wide, flat caps. Instead of carving, heart-shaped apertures long remained peculiarly popular ornamental detail together with continuing enjoyment of lettered mottoes and flat inlays of copper, pewter and stained glass.

Voysey enriched his simple oak with shapely metal mounts, but like his important fellow designers Christopher Dresser and W. A. S. Benson he was concerned to simplify design and accept cost-reducing machine processes.

From the 1890s many designers felt the urge to break away from tradition-bound academic styles with a wholly new approach to shape and ornament. But in furniture the new art or Art Nouveau was less extreme in England than on the Continent, with emphatic angular structure to contrast with inlaid or painted Art Nouveau ornament such as upthrusting plant growth—especially the wild rose—and intertwining leaves in vigorous whiplash curves.

Where carving is found this may be amateur work. For minor purposes stools, small tables and cabinets were amateur-ornamented with chip carving or with especially favoured poker work where the hot tool charred the background to produce relief effects. Much simple white wood furniture was sold for this early DIY. Cheap furniture was stained dull green or brown, and oak was 'fumed' to a dingy tone with ammonia. Now even this has acquired a look of venerable age.

Even before the end of the brief Edwardian period, however, the mood was changing. Avant garde designers of severe, rectilinear work for the few included exclusive Ernest Gimson and now favoured C. R. Mackintosh of Glasgow. But most influential perhaps was the furniture-maker Ambrose Heal whose gracious practical designs required no ornament save the beauty of fine light oak or chestnut wood.

Oak dressing table in an interesting design by Ambrose Heal typical of his carefully thought-out functional style. Text above.

Pottery

Fragments of pottery are among the earliest traces of ancient civilisations. In my next chapter I describe England's porcelains and renowned bone china, but here my concern is with all our other ceramic wares, usually recognised at a glance by being opaque. Collectors distinguish between the most easily kiln-fired earthenwares, porous to liquids until covered with glaze, and the stonewares heated until their ingredients become extremely hard and watertight.

Medieval Britain has left us treasured pieces of brownish earthenwares, but we can find many more brightly gleaming, time-defiant fragments to remind us how earthenwares developed in Georgian and Victorian days, giving us slipware, delftware, creamware, lustreware, Prattware and the rest. Early stonewares, brown, buff, red, black, white, were forerunners of such delicacies as Wedgwood jasperware.

Early potters shaped their clay vessels and then made them watertight by dusting with powered lead before baking in primitive ovens. Under the resultant clear yellowish glaze local clays baked to a range of colours–reds, greys, buff, cream–and this prompted the splendid uninhibited ornament on such early slipware as plates, posset pots, two-handled tygs and puzzle jugs. Patterns in contrasting colours were created by pressing strips or pads of clay on to their surface or by thinning the clay to the semi-fluid condition called slip and trailing this in bold freehand designs over the ware. Sometimes the warm-toned ware was coated in whitish slip so that patterns could be incised to show the colour beneath.

English delftware

Primitive slipware still flourished in Victorian days, but by the late 17th century fashion dictated Chinese white porcelain ornamented in blue. In attempted imitation many English potters followed the Netherlands with what became known as English delftware. The craft was brought to London tentatively as early as 1570. In the following century it became important in Southwark and Lambeth and extended to Bristol, Liverpool, Staffordshire and elsewhere. It was immensely attractive because the coarse buff-coloured earthenware was wholly hidden by a substantial smooth white covering opacified with costly tin oxide. Uninhibited freehand ornament was painted on this, ranging from loyal portraits of royalty to chinoiserie, and the glaze remained clear of slipware's yellow tinge.

Tin enamelled earthenware (English delftware) painted with a lady fishing. She wears a flowing yellow dress and the distant landscape is sketched in blue. Bristol. Text above.

Handsome stonewares

For workaday use, however, the potter wanted stronger wares, so he forced up the heat of his kilns until his earthy clay-sand mixture hardened into stoneware. Brown stoneware–drainpipe ware to many of us–has never gone out of use and was adored by aesthetic Victorians. Salt shovelled into the immensely hot kiln gave the ware a rough glaze. John Dwight founded his long-lived Fulham stoneware factory in 1671 making brown, white, red and a mottled 'agate' stoneware. Unglazed red stoneware is associated with the Elers brothers who came from Holland in 1658, setting a high standard for red teapots, lathe-trimmed and ornamented with motifs attached ('sprigged') to the surface before firing.

Red stoneware, too, continued through the 18th and 19th centuries, made by Wedgwood (rosso antico), Wood, Spode, Hollins among many others. Throughout the 18th century a wonderfully richly glowing brown with a metallic glint was known as Nottingham ware and associated especially with the Morley family, its surface enriched with an iron oxide slip. Some fine Morley vessels show incised decoration.

The 18th century's common black stoneware, known as Egyptian black, was a once-fired ware less important to collectors than improved black basaltes (page 34).

Agate ware cat with colour enhanced by touches of blue on head and body. Height $5\frac{1}{2}$ inches. About 1745. Text above. Victoria and Albert Museum, London.

Far more exciting to early Georgians was white stoneware. John Astbury (1686–1743) was, perhaps, the first potter to whiten his clay with crushed burnt flints: this gave him a creamy earthenware, but when fired at a higher temperature the white stoneware could almost pass for porcelain. It was difficult to throw on the wheel but was mould-shaped in all the bold fantastic patterns of early 18th-century silver. The salt-glazed surface was too rough for drinking vessels but was fine for other table wares, from teapots to pickle trays. Colour at first, from the 1720s, was limited to blue-stained powdered glass sprinkled into incisions before firing. Full-colour enamel painting in the porcelain manner followed from about 1750.

Early Georgian earthenwares were still coarse and fragile. The most interesting include reddish ware ornamented with raised white motifs and glossy black jetware, sometimes gold-enriched, associated with Jackfield, Shropshire, from 1751.

The 18th century saw spectacular developments in porcelain figure ornaments, but there is a special appeal about earthenware figures. By about the 1730s–1740s a few potters were beginning to shape prim little figures by finger-rolling and cutting their clay and dabbing in details such as beady eyes and coat buttons with contrasting coloured slip. John Astbury may possibly be credited with some early 'pew groups'. These have no religious significance, but the homely little men and women are supported by high-backed settles. Other figures in stoneware and earthenware were shaped in moulds and include musicians, soldiers and horsemen. Today these precious primitives are usually museum specimens–or the inevitable fakes.

The Astbury family remain elusive, but Thomas Whieldon, 1719–95, can be seen as an immensely important personality in the story of English pottery. All variegated (tortoiseshell and marbled) wares of his period and later tend to be known as Whieldon wares although made by Leeds, Liverpool and other Staffordshire potters. These attractive earthenwares were coloured with metallic oxides that flowed and mingled in irregular streaks and blotches in the clear lead glaze. He was in partnership with Josiah Wedgwood from 1754 to 1759, and among his apprentices was Josiah Spode. With Wedgwood he developed green-glazed and yellow-glazed wares and the green-and-creamy-yellow effects exploited in pots shaped to suggest cauliflowers, pineapples or sweetcorn.

Improved tablewares

World-famous Josiah Wedgwood, 1730–95, benevolent, autocratic industrialist, dominated the Staffordshire potteries. He created a workers' factory village and called it Etruria to show his approval of then-fashionable Neo-classicism. Among his earliest successes was his cream-coloured tableware, a refined earthenware dipped in liquid glaze. This was such a notable improvement that in 1765 Queen Charlotte allowed him to call it queen's ware. As might be expected Wedgwood was alert to the porcelain men's new notion of ornament quickly applied in great detail with paper transfers inked by etched copper plates. Much of his early creamware was sent to Sadler and Green of Liverpool, specialists in such one-colour printing from 1756.

Creamware was the first really pleasant everyday tableware and was potted from Staffordshire to Scotland, from Sunderland to Bristol and South Wales. Some especially fine work came

Spode blue and white teapot, 4 inches tall. The transfer-printed decoration is the *Milkmaid* pattern introduced in 1814. Text opposite page. Spode-Copeland Museum.

from the Leeds Pottery who made and catalogued and successfully exported many tablewares, very light in weight, with a glassy glaze. Some were painted in enamel colours like porcelain; other pieces were colour-glazed or transfer-printed or delicately pierced with hand punches. Much was left plain but given attractive double-twisted or crabstock (crab-apple twig) handles. Elsewhere in South Yorkshire, Leeds was closely associated with the Swinton pottery, later famous for Rockingham china, with the Don pottery and with Castleford, all sources, too, of stonewares.

Wedgwood was debarred by a bitterly contested monopoly from making 'true' porcelain but experimented endlessly to make really white pottery and in 1779 produced pearlware, an important white earthenware ideal for porcelain-style ornament in blue. To most of us 'Staffordshire blue' means useful white earthenwares richly covered with detailed pictures and borders in cobalt blue, applied under a protective clear glaze. Josiah Spode I, 1733–97, and his son were leaders in this underglaze transfer-printing which was brilliantly successful especially about 1810–40 in all the pottery regions of Britain. So clear were these printed patterns that the period could indulge to the full in its adored picturesque views and romantic buildings, in story scenes and such imagined chinoiserie as the undying willow pattern.

Wedgwood jasperware

Wedgwood and his partner Bentley (*d.* 1780) issued earthenware ornaments too, in finely proportioned Neo-classical shapes such as vase and urn, table lamp and inkstand. Some were colour-glazed to suggest marble or porphyry. But he is remembered especially for his velvety matt-surfaced fine-stonewares, known by some collectors as dry stonewares. These required no glaze and permitted the quality of detail that he admired in Greco-Roman gem-carving for making portrait cameos and decorative bas reliefs in the Neo-classical manner. To most of us the name Wedgwood immediately suggests that delicate pale blue jasperware, evolved about 1774 and in production still, its matt surface patterned with low relief figures mould-shaped separately in white jasperware and sprigged on before firing. From 1785 the white jasper might be coloured merely on the surface (jasper dip) in the restrained muted colours we associate with this extremely hard stoneware.

Collectors look not only for the usual range of vessels but for bas relief panels inserted in chimneypiece and cabinet in the Neo-classical fashion. Wedgwood commissioned leading designers such as John Flaxman, R.A., and sentimental scenes from Lady Templetown and Lady Di Beauclerk.

Black basaltes (the modern ware is known as basalt) was Wedgwood's improvement from the 1760s on the period's common black stoneware. It was twice-fired to a wonderful glowing black and used for great numbers of fashionable busts, bas reliefs, plaques and sets of small medallions. Subjects extended from classical statesmen and writers to modern heroes. So fine was the basaltes surface that it could be engraved mechanically in the delicate patterns of closely spaced lines known as engine turning.

The creamy buff fine-stoneware called caneware was exploited in vessels shaped to suggest strips of bamboo lashed with cane. Caneware vessels realistically shaped as appetising pastry pies were popular too around the end of the 18th century when war conditions required economies in the vast spread of dishes expected at a smart dinner. In this as in all his fine-stonewares Wedgwood had a number of rivals: for example, collectors seek jasper and basaltes marked by Adams, Turner, Mayer and Neale.

Wood figures and Toby jugs

In the late 18th century the not-so-rich indulged happily in endless 'shams' to suggest wealth and grandeur including splendid pottery figures to mimic exquisite porcelain. Ralph Wood, 1715–72, and his son of the same name, 1748–95, marked some work and so can be associated with the development of figures including such character jugs as the familiar Toby. Related Aaron Wood and his son Enoch, 1759–1840, were important too, Enoch being a fine modeller of large, vivid portrait figures. The Wood *Vicar-and-Moses* group was still being reproduced in the early 1960s.

The important colour change in later 18th-century figures was from Whieldon-type mingled colours, first to controlled brush-applied colour glazes and then to the porcelain-maker's overglaze painted enamels. Some coarse unsmiling faces are associated with the efficient but wayward modeller John Voyez who probably worked from 1770 to 1790 for the Woods.

Voyez signed one familiar jug design shaped as lovers at a tree stump and this type of earthenware moulded with figures in deep relief was extremely popular from about the 1790s, including plaques, jugs and so on. Projecting ornament especially needed glaze applied over the colours: so-called Prattware was decorated entirely in the limited range of crude 'high temperature' colours that could stand the kiln heat of subsequent glazing, including blue, yellow, purple, brownish orange and red.

Earthenware figure group by Enoch Wood entitled *The Vicar and Moses*. This was still being modelled in the 1960s. Text above.

Lustres and other cottage wares

By then of course there was colour in plenty for the earthenware collector, none more appealing today than the everyday wares thickly covered with iridescent metallic lustres. Strangely, although this ware was a new process, simpler than renowned early Hispano-Moresque lustres and was made by innumerable early 19th-century English potters, it is seldom marked. Oily solutions of metallic salts were thinly washed over the wares, appearing as bright guinea gold or a deeper gold or silver or pinkish purple.

Use of dark red earthenware gave the gold a coppery tone; pinkish shades came from gold-and-tin; silver from untarnishing platinum, made steely dark by adding manganese. Wedgwood made quantities of a blotchy 'moonlight lustre'. Sometimes the ware was entirely covered with lustre to suggest a vessel of silver or gold, even to the beaded rims, but thicker of course than metal. But more often the potter left reserves for painted decoration.

So-called resist lustre was patterned with a substance that would repel the metallic solution so that it adhered only where there was no resist, most usually forming a background to leaf and bird ornament. Another distinctive type was known as Sunderland although made also elsewhere. This covered the ware with a bubbled, splashed effect in purplish or reddish gold. It may be found on jugs printed with views of Sunderland's Wearmouth bridge and other simple gift pottery such as frog mugs and widely bordered text plaques.

Silver resist lustre serving jugs. About 1810. Text above.

Streaky chocolate-brown glaze with a wonderful sheen was also popular for cottagey wares far into the 19th century. This was made throughout England and Scotland but was long known as Rockingham glaze and associated with the Rockingham pottery. Here they mixed the lead glaze with manganese oxide to a lustrous purple-brown and applied it thickly by repeated dippings on to red earthenware vessels such as pots and Toby jugs. The so-called Cadogan teapot may be found, said to be derived from a Chinese wine pot. This lacks a lid opening, being filled through a spiralling tube in the base. Glossy black jetware was popular too and cheap black fireclay ware for massive wine coolers and conservatory urns.

Collectable teapots

Tea became cheaper and teapots more varied in the early 19th century, and they are found in many interesting shapes and styles, from bamboo ware to basaltes and white stoneware. The Castleford stoneware teapot is distinctive, characterised by a vertical collar around the lid and vertical ribs between slightly concave panels containing moulded reliefs. Felspathic stonewares fired at very high temperatures, strong and heat-retaining, became widely important at this time. Castleford was but one of many firms that met the need for stronger domestic wares with 'stone china', 'new stone', 'semi-porcelain', 'Saxon stone' and the like, made and marked by Adams, Spode, Davenport, Meigh and many others. William Ridgway, for example, was one of many potters issuing notable all-white stoneware jugs with boldly moulded figure scenes, comparable with the jugs in parian ware that I shall mention later among early Victorian porcelains. In contrast the Mason firm lavished colourful confused 'Japan' patterns on a hard white earthenware that they called patent ironstone china. This was made into articles ranging from the familiar sets of octagonal jugs to fireplaces.

Lava ware was yet another heavy, strong cottage ware. Collectors of these once-cheap wares delight in the popular mug containing a frog climbing up inside towards the drinker's mouth. Other collectors seek out shellfish measures and a wide range of jugs and kitchen wares banded with cheap underglaze decoration consisting of fine wavering lines suggesting ferns or moss. This was known as mocha-ware. Any factory child could turn and twist the vessel while a blob of acid-based colour diffused through a band of wet clay slip.

Figures and flatbacks

Coarse brown stoneware was still in demand too for workaday Brampton (Derbyshire) hunting jugs with relief-moulded country scenes and greyhound handles. Spirit flasks were made too by Doulton and other firms for pub use topped by head-and-shoulders busts, often of political heroes, around the 1820s–1840s. But for chimney shelf in villa and well furnished cottage the early 19th century could offer far more colourful ornaments. Guileless figures cheaply potted in brittle earthenware provided endless illustrations of long-loved Biblical stories and offered homesick recruits to the factory towns reminders of the sentiment, humour, even the animals of their country childhood.

John Walton, at work about 1806–35, gave his figures crude little bocage backgrounds of oak leaves, to suggest the flowery bowers or bocages that supported many porcelain groups. His work might be impressed WALTON on the tall base, but this may be found on reproductions. Ralph Salt, 1782–1846, made figures in a similar style, as did Thomas Rathbone of Portobello, Edinburgh, about 1808–50. Among others, Obadiah Sherratt, 1776–1840s, produced ambitious groups often with a streak of robust humour. Typically the base had four feet linked by a wavy frieze and was coloured to suggest marble. Many other splendid little figures came from Sunderland including some of the spotted lustre dogs loved by early Victorians.

By the 1840s, however, the vogue had begun for what are known as Victorian flatbacks. For cheapness the figure was often shaped in a single somewhat tapering mould, the back left plain, the front quickly hand painted. Innumerable named 'portraits' sold on their topicality. Colour details such as royalty's ermine dots might aid recognition but as the ware became whiter, brilliantly glazed, colour became minimal. Use of a bright gilding known as liquid gold began in 1853, but the collector can date most specimens by subject or dress—and must be extremely wary of reproductions.

A similar naive commentary on passing events delights the collector of picture pot-lids, but here the process consisted of a highly sophisticated development of full-colour transfer-printing. This was evolved by Jesse Austin, 1806–79, working for F. and R. Pratt. The small round white pots were originally sold filled with hair pomades, fish pastes and the like. The lids were slightly rounded after 1848. Many have been reissued.

Pot-lid pictures followed current taste with story-telling themes (the early scenes of bears being associated with bear's grease hair pomade). But critics bewailed the gulf between art and industrial ornament, shown for example by the 1851 Great Exhibition. Even talented well-intentioned artists tended to paint inappropriate pictures on vase and pilgrim bottle, and designers knew little of craft techniques. Herbert Minton, how-

Pot lid printed with a popular scene *Bears at School* (by F. and R. Pratt and Co.). This picture is found with varying detail and in a re-issue. Text above.
Mrs M. Stephens.

ever, won wide success from 1848 by employing French Léon Arnoux, 1816–1902, chemist, potter and eventually art director.

Among Minton-Arnoux successes were majolica, Palissy ware and 'Henri II' inlaid pottery. His majolica, widely imitated, was mould-shaped in deep relief ornament and covered with rich heavily leaded colour glazes. Articles ranged from fireplaces to ladies' work-baskets, from figures to cheese stands.

Victorian art pottery

Minton's was one of the few firms using impressed yearly date symbols. The Victorians' much-used registration marks are explained on page 61. But many of the later 19th century's most interesting items date themselves by their fascinating reflections of the strengths and limitations of the new craft-conscious aesthetes.

Doulton's of Lambeth produced some early 19th century commemorative stonewares, but the firm was mainly important for domestic and industrial wares until the 1860s when the Lambeth School of Art collaborated in art wares. Hard brown stoneware for example, from clock cases to chessmen, was

This page: Doulton art pottery. *Left:* salt-glazed stoneware vase by William Parker, about 1890. *Right:* Lambeth faience vase painted with flowers by Minna Crawley, 1879. Text opposite page.

Opposite page: Typical designs by William de Morgan. *Left:* vase made at Fulham, 1888–98. *Centre:* Staffordshire earthenware plate probably painted at Merton Abbey, 1882–8. *Right:* an early Merton Abbey piece painted in 'Persian' colours. Text page 42. Victoria and Albert Museum, London.

variously coloured, stamped and carved before being once-fired–including salt glazing–along with common domestic wares. The matt white surface of another stoneware inspired the name carrara ware. Silicon stoneware, with a trace of glaze, was incised, stamped and patterned with raised slip. Marqueterie ware suggested the tiny squares of wood veneer used by the Tunbridge marquetry men, but with the decoration formed in mosaics of coloured clay. Chiné ware was given a textured fabric surface by pressing net into the unfired clay.

Some valuable Doulton work is artist-signed or initialled. Artist designs carried out by students may be marked X. Several kinds of earthenware were ornamented too. For example, some Doulton artists painted and gilded pilgrim bottles and the like in a fine clay-coloured earthenware called Lambeth faience (more costly Crown Lambeth from 1892).

Terracotta was rediscovered by early Victorians, especially for conservatory ware. This soft earthenware, unglazed and porous, ranged in colour from glowing red to yellow and brown, its slightly glossy surface well suited to painting in the approved ancient Etruscan manner. Ambitious terracotta relief panels, such as Biblical scenes, were created at Doulton's from 1886 by George Tinworth, 1843–1913.

Also in the London area, the four Martin brothers ran their own stoneware studio pottery at Southall, 1877–1915. They used many colours and surface textures but are remembered especially now for grotesques such as Walter's Wally bird tobacco jars.

Here again the late Victorian period offered wonderful opportunities to individual talent, and many artist-potters became absorbed in experiments with skilfully manipulated colour glazes. Inventive, brilliant William de Morgan, 1839–1917, close friend of William Morris, created satisfying two-dimensional patterns in intense metallic lustres and 'Persian' blues and greens. Rich colours contained within artist-incised outlines are found in the fully initialled but somewhat casually finished work of Harold Rathbone's Della Robbia Pottery, at Birkenhead, 1894–1906. At Minton's, Leon Solon combined moulded and slip-trailed outlines with flowing colour to ornament his Art Nouveau Secessionist ware from 1902.

Splendid streaky colour glazes fascinated many late Victorian and Edwardian studio potters—at Linthorpe near Middlesbrough, for example, at Swadlincote and Bretby in Derbyshire and at Burmantofts in Leeds. Here spilly iridescent glaze colours dominated the bold, sometimes eccentric Oriental and Art Nouveau shapes. The remarkably forward-looking Christopher Dresser left his name on some striking vessels made at Linthorpe and Swadlincote. As a professional designer he was associated too with late Victorian metalwork and Scottish Clutha glass.

Working into the early 20th century, William Moorcroft is remembered for rich colours subtly blended in patterns of fruit and leaf. Howson Taylor at the Ruskin Pottery, Smethwick, won lasting admiration for a range of splashed and intensely coloured glazes, iridescent lustres and mottled effects. At Pilkington's Lancastrian Pottery near Manchester too a team of artists produced strikingly decorative effects with opalescent glazes and scintillating lustres.

More difficult to date are some Victorian traditional country wares such as green-glazed earthenware harvest jugs by the Fishley family of Fremington, Devon. More sophisticated country wares, all too prone to the period's 'quaintness', were made at Barnstable, at Devonshire's thriving Aller Vale Potteries and most notably at Clevedon by the wide-ranging, self-taught Sir Edmund Elton.

Sussex is associated with hen-and-chickens (nest egg) money-pots and the Sussex pig dividing at the neck into jug and cup. Some Rye vessels were decorated with separately shaped hop sprays, but more elaborate primitive motifs were attached all about the huge brown 'barge' teapots of the South Derbyshire area. These were sometimes individually named and dated. On the idiosyncratic pottery of Castle Hedingham, Essex, 1864–1905, the sprigged-on motifs might include 17th-century dates and references to Essex history.

One collectable item I have scarcely mentioned is the pottery tile. Collectors quickly realise that these perfectly represent many of the different styles and moods of all the periods in this book. Victorians especially were delighted by the possibilities of wall tiles. These date mainly to the second half of the century when they were made by such firms as Minton Copeland, Doulton, Maw and very many others including outstanding art potters such as De Morgan. Not least of their attractions is the fact that the collector may still occasionally acquire them direct from the wall or alcove where once they were considered essential adornment in fashionable theatre, shop or home.

Wall plate from the Della Robbia Pottery, Birkenhead. Artists' marks: G incised; two Gs, one reversed, in colour. At this art pottery it was customary for different decorators to incise and colour the ornament. Text page 42. Watkin-Garratt collection.

Porcelain and Bone China

Milk and honey–symbols of health, wealth and happiness–are represented charmingly on some of England's earliest porcelain, the goat-and-bee jugs made by the porcelain factory at Chelsea. A pair of drowsy goats lie head-to-tail supporting a jug with a rustic handle and relief decoration of flowers and a magnificent bee.

Other vessels were shaped as leaves or shells or patterned in relief with prunus sprays. This is typical of England's approach to porcelain, inspired by silverware to give a touch of flowery fantasy to useful wares that at last could attempt to challenge the gleaming porcelains imported from China. Such pioneer English work was produced from the 1740s: by the early 1750s well-to-do sophisticates could enjoy the porcelains of at least six rival English factories.

These were the firms whose famous names are the pride of our museums, their work smoothly glazed, translucent, fashionably decorative–but only a little less fragile than contemporary ornaments in earthenware.

A porcelain plate held against the light shows one's fingers darkly through its translucent texture: that generally is the essential difference between porcelain and usually opaque earthenwares. The secret of how to make the hard glossy porcelain of China long remained in the Orient, and shipments to Europe were avidly collected by the well-to-do. At Meissen near

Dresden from about 1708 potters used the Chinese ingredients, basically derived from felspar rock, blending and shaping the paste, covering the vessels in glaze and firing them in an intensely hot kiln so that they emerged hard, glossy and translucent. Blue ornament could be painted under the glaze, but most other colours were added over it, being fixed by a gentler heat.

This, it must be stressed, was porcelain as the Chinese knew it. England in the 1740s–1750s (and France, too, at this time) accepted instead an imitation, making their clay paste translucent by mixing in glass ingredients (frit) and kiln-firing it at a more moderate temperature. Hence the names frit porcelain and soft paste porcelain. The hard paste porcelain of China, imitated at Meissen and later elsewhere in Europe, was made only briefly in 18th-century England.

Chelsea shepherd in brilliantly coloured costume against flowering branches and mounted on elaborate gilded scroll–all details typical of the firm's gold anchor period. Text page 46.

Chelsea's changing moods

Mellow, soft paste porcelain with a creamy glaze is found in table wares, ornaments and engaging small personal items such as figure scent bottles. Chelsea especially is renowned for these. This pioneer factory was in production from about 1745, marking some early wares with an incised triangle. Subsequently anchor marks were used. A 'raised' anchor on a moulded pad dated to about 1749–53; a very tiny red anchor to 1753–56; and an equally inconspicuous gold anchor to 1758–69. All have been faked on other porcelains, but museums offer a chance to see real Chelsea porcelain, to enjoy the restrained beauty of form and ornament through the middle period and the colourful gilded magnificence that followed.

Bow, Derby, Worcester and their rivals

Chelsea's early all-white porcelain figures contrast strikingly with later flower-decked groups. An early rival of similar charm was London's Bow factory, though again the exact starting date is unknown. With Chinese imports in mind the factory from 1749 was called New Canton, and the name is found on souvenir inkwells. This firm too was famed for finely painted table wares in Chinese mood such as an engaging pattern of two small plump partridges. Their blue-painted wares were among the finest of their day, and they made attractive flowery-costumed figures, often raised on high scrolling pedestals.

An important rival was Derby. This factory made porcelain from about 1749, but came to the fore from 1756. William Duesbury was then in control using a glossy soft paste porcelain with a thick white glaze for figures, ornaments and table wares.

Most elusive of these early porcelain factories was Longton Hall, Staffordshire, at work 1749–60 making tea, coffee and dessert services, flowery candlesticks and vases, elaborate figures and many simple little pieces such as pickle dishes shaped as leaves and mugs with handles in fanciful loops. William Littler, manager from 1751, is remembered for the rich ultramarine 'Littler's blue'. Recent research has suggested the existence of other minor porcelain factories, both in Chelsea and near Longton Hall.

Bristol, about 1749–52, had a factory making table wares and rare figures in soft paste porcelain, not to be confused with its later better known hard paste porcelain. Here too one glimpses how mid 18th-century potters struggled to strengthen their fine-looking wares. Bow pioneered by adding animal bone as an ingredient. At Bristol and Worcester Cornish soapstone or steatite was introduced. This soapstone porcelain was heavier but made sturdier, heat-resistant table wares.

Worcester used soapstone to such good effect that their teapots are renowned. Here again one can trace the development of an important firm, beginning about 1751 with well-potted domestic wares, neatly painted in blue under the glaze and advancing in the 1760s to more ambitious work in brilliant colours. Fantastic 'japan patterns' imitating Oriental imports became especially rich and brilliant at Worcester. Delicate line work in gold over magnificent coloured grounds was popular too, often surrounding exotic birds in landscapes painted on shapely vases, although for some of this work the white porcelain was bought by London china decorators. The Worcester works museum has many on view.

Bow porcelain dinner plate hand painted in underglaze blue. This dates to about 1760 when Bow was renowned for some of Europe's finest blue and white ware. Text opposite page. Victoria and Albert Museum, London.

Liverpool and Lowestoft

Worcester served the West Midlands and holiday travellers, including the Royal family in 1788 when the firm became the Royal Worcester Porcelain Co. In the north-west Liverpool had its own potteries, several making soft paste porcelain until late 18th-century canals brought competition from the Staffordshire potteries. William Reid was one of the first, and Chaffers, Christian and Pennington were among Liverpool's leading manufacturers in the 1750s–1770s, some of their soft porcelain containing either bone ash or soapstone.

Much handsome table ware came from Liverpool, such as punch bowls, punch pots (like teapots but without strainers) and 'silver shape' sauce boats. But one-colour ornament quickly printed in fine detail from transfer papers, first used on the porcelains of Bow and Worcester, was successful, too, at Liverpool.

Blue ornament on white porcelain is so attractive that we must be thankful that English potters, like the Chinese before them, found it the most easily managed colour for everyday wares, including transfer printing. It could be applied before the glazing that protected it from scratches but was difficult to

Liverpool porcelain punch bowl. Painted in enamels in full colour with the sailing ship *The Swallow*. About 1765. Text above. Victoria and Albert Museum, London.

paint smoothly as a background. Lowestoft, like Bow, sprayed it on the ware.

Lowestoft, 1757–*c.* 1800, met local needs by painting views, even names and birth dates, at customers' request and making souvenir wares much treasured today. But their workaday ware has no association whatever with the imported Chinese porcelain painted to commission with heraldic motifs that has acquired the name of 'armorial Lowestoft'.

Later 18th-century splendour

Soft paste porcelain factories continued to contribute important ornaments and table wares through the later 18th century, inspired still by Continental hard paste porcelain, with German Meissen now less favoured than French Sèvres. (Both French and German porcelain makers tried to stop Bow and Chelsea imports.) An outstanding figure was William Duesbury, 1725–86, who began as a London porcelain decorator but, with partners, acquired the Derby factory in 1756, Chelsea in 1769 and Bow in 1776. He made Derby porcelain some of the finest in England, with a restrained grace of design and well painted ornament such as landscapes and botanical specimens. 'Chelsea Derby' figures, lavish, sentimental, date to 1770–84 when Duesbury at Derby employed highly skilled craftsmen from Chelsea. At the Chelsea factory Duesbury revived manufacture of the tiny figure scent bottles, seals and other fashionable 'toys' that collectors most treasure today.

Another important porcelain maker was engraver Thomas Turner, 1749–1809, who left Worcester to establish the Salopian China Manufactory at Caughley (pronounced Carfley) near Broseley, Shropshire, in 1775. There has been much confusion between Worcester's and Caughley's heat-resistant soapstone porcelain. Table wares, such as mask jugs, were often painted and transfer-printed in very similar blue patterns, as for instance the charming chinoiserie *Fisherman*. Caughley was acquired in 1799 by John Rose of Coalport.

At Worcester, too, there were changes. The most famous

Chelsea-Derby ewers in the Neo-classical manner. The borders are of Smith's blue, and the figure subjects by Askew. Gold anchor mark. About 1780. Text page 49.

early years known as the Dr Wall or Wall-Davis period ended in 1793 when Thomas Flight took charge. Magnificent vases were painted and much splendid table ware. A typical tea service would include a lidded tea canister and a spoon tray, but only 12 saucers for its 12 tea bowls and 12 coffee cups.

Another Worcester decorator, Robert Chamberlain, left the Worcester factory in 1783 and with his son became successful first in decorating and then in making fine porcelain, receiving many prestige orders such as armorial dinner services. Thomas Grainger started yet another china works in Worcester in 1801.

White bisque ornaments

Worcester's gorgeous ornaments in rich colours and gold contrast with another pleasure of the 1780s–1790s: delicately detailed bisque porcelain, associated especially with Derby. Figures in once-fired soft paste porcelain 'biscuit' were given a satiny sheen by minimal glazing (called smear glazing) and sold in-the-white; less perfect pieces were coloured in the usual way. But far more white ornaments remain from the 19th century, in chalky white china and Victorian parian ware.

Hard paste porcelain

Some of England's finest hard paste porcelain, too, was left 'in-the-white', including the plaques made only at Bristol, decorated with coats of arms and exquisite little flowers in relief. This hard paste porcelain venture began at Plymouth in 1768 when Bristol chemist William Cookworthy at last, in Cornwall, found and monopolised ingredients such as the Chinese used for their porcelain. In 1770 he moved the enterprise to Bristol. The heat-resistant hard paste porcelain was well suited to tea-ware, but much shows the imperfections of a new manufacture and is simply blue-painted under the glaze. In 1773, however, Richard Champion developed the works more ambitiously, producing figures and ornaments in the Sèvres manner as well as the familiar barrel-shaped teapots.

Fashion, alas, preferred to obtain such wares from the Continent, and in 1778 Champion went bankrupt. He sold his patent to a group of Staffordshire potters who in 1781 launched the New Hall China Manufactory, Shelton. The outcome was a range of china table wares in attractive simple shapes comparable with the period's silver, such as straight-sided teapots and helmet cream jugs. Lively informal ornament–flower sprigs and posies, chinoiseries, simple landscapes–is in the earthenware manner familiar to the firm's founders.

At New Hall even the porcelain itself, it seems, was a compromise, with the English potter's traditional methods of glazing applied to the hard paste ware. The practical potters accepted further compromise in 1812, making the form of porcelain known as bone china until about 1835.

The first quarter of the 19th century was a notable period for enterprising English potters of table wares, for from 1794 Continental imports were greatly restricted. Among the finest wares evolved then was felspar porcelain made by Josiah Spode II from about 1800 for costly table wares, brilliantly white and flawless. Coalport made this too. At Worcester, Chamberlain made his brilliantly translucent Regent china, about 1811–20. But when the Worcester firms combined as Chamberlain and Co. in 1840 the typical far-famed English porcelain was the strong translucent ware we know today as bone china.

World-renowned bone china

This is so important that its history is worth recalling. The man mainly responsible was Josiah Spode, 1733–97, an important innovator at his Stoke-upon-Trent pottery from 1770. Champion's extended monopoly of the Cornish ingredients for porcelain ended in 1796. By then Spode was ready to launch his china, consisting of the Cornish hard porcelain ingredients together with large quantities of animal bone ash. Other potters were quick to develop this great new enterprise, among the first being the Minton firm, Derby, Coalport, both Chamberlain and

Spode pot-pourri vase. This has a perforated lid to release the perfume and also an inner cover to retain it when required. The ornament is a typically vivid japan pattern. About 1815. Text above.

Grainger of Worcester, John Davenport, and the Herculaneum Pottery at Liverpool. New Hall began in 1812; Wedgwood made it 1812–22 and again from 1878.

Josiah Spode's similarly named son and grandson continued the firm until 1829 when control went to W. T. Copeland, whose marks include *Copeland and Garrett* (1833–47) and others incorporating the name Spode. Before 1820 there were more than twenty makers of bone china. Most ware was unmarked, but even when a mark is found it is often no more than a pattern number or name; this meant that a replacement could be ordered from the china seller who liked to keep his sources secret.

John Rose of Coalport, 1773–1828, was an important maker of bone china wares such as delightful flower-encrusted ornaments. Among seldom recorded claims to fame is his invention of a glaze free of the lead that poisoned innumerable potters.

Rose's son and great-nephew continued the Coalport pottery through the 19th century, but there are many problems for the Coalport collector. Much of their early bone china was decorated in London. Towards the mid century their brilliant bone china imitations of Continental work might be given Sèvres or Chelsea marks. The familiar mark COALPORT A.D. 1750 (the year claimed for the start of their predecessor Caughley) was introduced in the 1860s, and at this time the firm added glazed ornament to many years' accumulation of once fired 'biscuit' china.

Derby, with Robert Bloor in command from about 1812, is associated with bone china that shows cost-cutting gaudy ornament. But here again there are problems, for he too used up old stocks including late 18th-century soft paste porcelain. The works closed in 1848 but was soon reopened, the most important proprietor being Sampson Hancock. Collectors must realise that his mark, the letters SH flanking a crown and crossed swords, much like older Derby marks, was used until 1935. Fine bone china was made too by the Derby Crown Porcelain Co., established 1876, which became 'Royal Crown Derby' in 1890.

When John Davenport died in 1836 he had 1400 employees and a thriving export trade in high quality bone china lavishly gilded. Another prosperous china seller, Miles Mason, made china from about 1800 after the high import tariff of 1794 cut off Continental porcelain supplies. But he retired – rich – in 1813, his wares overshadowed now by his sons' famous 'patent ironstone china' which was a fine earthenware.

Brilliant Billingsley and Randall

The gay glitter of this thriving trade in upstart bone china prompted new efforts from the traditionalists to fashion England's long-loved soft paste porcelains into more exotic wares. Wealthy Regency and late Georgian collectors sought especially the 'old Sèvres' French soft paste porcelain, rarer than the usual hard paste Sèvres. This involved indirectly two remarkable men, William Billingsley, 1758–1828, and Thomas Randall, 1786–1859.

Billingsley is associated with exquisitely soft-textured flowers painted on other firms' porcelains, including Derby, but his goal was to make his own porcelain as perfect as early Sèvres. With great skill but too little capital he tried again and again, at Pinxton, Brampton-in-Torksey and most notably at Swansea and Nantgarw. He ended, still dissatisfied, as a decorator at Coalport.

Billingsley's best porcelain was too difficult to make as an economical proposition, but some fine pieces remain. His friend Randall worked in London decorating porcelain for the china seller Mortlock until about 1825. Then he established himself at Madeley near Coalport, receiving poorly decorated Sèvres porcelain and transforming it into the lavishly coloured and gilded old Sèvres sought by collectors. It has been suggested that he also made soft paste porcelain, but scarcely any Madeley work was marked. Randall brilliantly imitated the Sèvres coloured grounds, the Watteau-esque scenes, landscapes, chinoiseries and lavish gilding, but he withstood every persuasion by the china sellers to add Sèvres marks.

Costly Rockingham

Billingsley's first concern was the white porcelain itself, often sent to London for decorating; Randall sought merely a porcelain paste worthy of his ornament. Less perfect than Nantgarw, less exotic than Randall-Sèvres, the luxury ware we now associate with the 1820s–1830s is the bone china produced, about 1826–41, by a Yorkshire pottery on the Rockingham estate of Earl Fitzwilliam. This was a long-established earthenware factory, but when they launched into bone china the Brameld brothers obtained the Earl's patronage and indulged in hopelessly costly extravagance; one dinner service cost William IV £5,000 and still proved unprofitable. Now, any piece with the famous Rockingham griffin mark is treasured, such as a coronet-finialed teapot or flower-encrusted scent bottle. But collectors no longer accept most of the period's unmarked flamboyant, graceless ornament long attributed to the firm.

Rediscovering Minton

Through research among old pattern books much unmarked ware, long attributed to Rockingham or Coalport, has been recognised as Minton work, and it has been possible to date, for example, the changing shapes and patterns of early tea ware. As yet, however, the firm seldom gains credit for its flower-

Minton basket of flowers and fruit, illustrated in their pattern book design number 72, but often assumed to be Coalport. Between 1826 and 1850. Text above.

encrusted ornaments, or for its figures including some in-the-white that may be misnamed Derby *bisque*. This important firm –Mintons from 1872–was launched by Thomas Minton, 1765–1836, one-time engraver at Caughley. He was followed by his son Herbert, 1792–1858, making bone china (brilliantly imitating Sèvres ornament), hard paste porcelain and white figures in parian porcelain as well as experimental earthenwares. Impressed yearly date symbols were introduced in 1842.

Notable lesser-known firms

Minton was a keen rival to the Spode-Copeland firm, but these giants had many other competitors. The Ridgways of Shelton, for example, made extremely sturdy bone china, often proudly marked with the royal arms and *JR & Co.* These included cabinet ornaments as well as colourful table wares.

The florid style loved by Victorians and too often attributed to Rockingham may often be the work of S. Alcock, active 1828–59, or of G. F. Bowers who made many a set of 'rustic' teapot, cream jug, sugar pot and the rest with handles shaped as branches ('crabstock') and feet as sprawling Rococo scrolls. But Alcock was among the early Victorian potters who also met another mood of the day–the utterly different interest in classical art.

Many potters throughout this period produced finely shaped ornaments in formal vase and urn designs and frequently described as Etruscan. But natural flower shapes predominated, none lovelier than those made at Belleek, Co. Fermanagh, N. Ireland, from the 1850s. Flowers in full relief might trail over baskets and covered bowls composed of delicate lattice work, but the major Belleek ornament was marine life. This was prompted by the use of a white matt-surfaced porcelain paste partly covered by a pearly iridescent glaze. Tea sets and other table wares could be made of extreme thinness and delicacy because exceptionally pure porcelain materials were locally available. Less fragile wares were evolved in the 1880s.

W. H. Goss of Stoke-on-Trent from 1858 made paper-thin tea

ware with paste and glaze closely resembling Belleek. But he is remembered especially for some of the other minor porcelain notions that appealed to innovation-loving Victorians, such as his flower jewellery from 1872—brooches, earrings, and so on, pure white or naturalistically tinted. He also made successful jewelled porcelain. This was stronger than the French and more elaborate than the jewelling of his English rivals who created rich effects with raised dots of coloured enamels. Goss heraldic china, which was his son's end-of-century creation, was widely imitated.

Important parian wares

Parian porcelain, basis of Belleek and Goss wares, was the most important early Victorian introduction, much used from 1842 by Copeland, Minton and other major potters. This form of felspar porcelain, ivory white with a delicate surface bloom suggesting Parian marble, was extremely popular for small statuary. Subjects ranged from classical figures to royal portraits and charming sentimental children with their pets. Important artists made the original models and moulds taken from these could turn out any number of copies. Some were distributed as minor prizes among subscribers to the Art-Union lotteries held annually in London and some provincial cities. Marks on parian figures sometimes refer to these. But even today such work is often mistaken for individually sculptured marble.

A cheaper form of parian porcelain was used for ornamental domestic wares. These included many of the white jugs decorated in deep relief, often with story themes, that are a source of special delight to collectors of mid 19th-century Victoriana.

Most of us probably share a little of the Victorians' eagerness to marvel. Porcelain lace for a Victorian figure of Ophelia, or Cleopatra, is exquisite nonsense associated with Minton, Grainger and others, using an old Rouen technique. Machine-made lace was soaked in cream-like porcelain slip and burnt away when the ornament was kiln-fired, leaving its pattern in the ware.

This page: Parian porcelain bust, *The Veiled Bride* after Raffaelle Monti. This was made by the Copeland firm, successors to Spode, as one of the prizes awarded in considerable numbers to participants in one of the art lotteries then popular: this one was run by the Crystal Palace Art Union. Height 15 inches. 1861. Text page 57. Mary Ireland collection.

Opposite page: Mid Victorian ornament. Left to right: 'Limoges enamel' style painted by Thomas Bott on Royal Worcester porcelain in 1867. Wall plate painted by Emile Lessore for Wedgwood in 1861. Covered bowl, Copeland, 1862. Snake-handled vase designed by Alfred Stevens for Minton, 1864. Text opposite page. Victoria and Albert Museum, London.

Another small Continental marvel was the lithophane, made by such English firms as Minton and Grainger. This is usually found today as a small plaque of glassy porcelain, its back so irregularly surfaced that when held against the light the hollows and bumps reveal a picture in light and shade. Lampshades were made and nightlight shelters and even teacups with surprise lithophane bases.

By the 1870s–1880s Victorians paid highly for another form of parian ornament made by several potters. This was pâte-sur-pâte—a wet creamy slip of the porcelain paste applied as decoration on the unfired dark-tinted paste of plaque or vase or pilgrim bottle. The paste was translucent when thin, but as layer after layer was added and dried the whiteness intensified. Delicate tooling completed the cameo effect before the piece was glazed and fired. Each item was a unique art work. Most famous maker was M. L. Solon who brought the ancient technique from Sèvres to Minton's.

Cameo effects were achieved at Worcester, too, most notably by Thomas Bott, with what were known as Limoges enamels. Here the rich blue ground was glazed and fired before being ornamented with slightly translucent white enamel, delicately painted layer upon layer and fixed by another firing.

Worcester at this period contributed especially notably to the new vogue for Japanese ornament, using fine ivory-tinted parian porcelain softly glazed and often decorated in gold and bronze. The firm used parian porcelain too for their glowing, subtly coloured Sabrina ware, patented 1894, with shadowy decoration in Art Nouveau patterns. Another turn-of-the-century success here was the pierced ware by George Owen, perforated with extraordinary delicacy before firing.

Makers' marks

In this far-too-brief summary I cannot even begin to describe other late Victorian delights such as the extremely rich effects of lacy gilded patterns in low relief. Many pieces show makers' marks which help to tell their own story.

Symbols used by leading 18th-century makers are interesting but often appear on fakes and imitations, old and new. 19th-century marks, when used, are more helpful, especially with dating. For example, Worcester, Minton, Derby and Wedgwood were among the leading firms who used date symbols changing each year. Many more firms registered their patterns to protect them from copyists. Between 1842 and 1883 the British Patent

Royal Worcester porcelain dish, 1912–1914. From a dessert set painted with a series of birds in their natural settings, signed by the renowned bird painter James Stinton. Text above.

Office used a Registry mark on British manufactured goods. The mark shows the exact year, month and date of an object. The year letters run in a sequence from 1842 to 1867 as follows: X, H, C, A, I, F, U, S, V, P, D, Y, J, E, L, K, B, M, Z, R, O, G, N, W, Q, T. In 1868 the mark was changed slightly and the sequence of letters started again and ran from X in 1868 to K in 1883. The months were indicated by the letters C, G, W, H, E, M, I, R, D, B, K, A. R was used for 1st–19th September 1857, K for December 1860, and G for 1st–6th March 1878, the latter with W for the year.

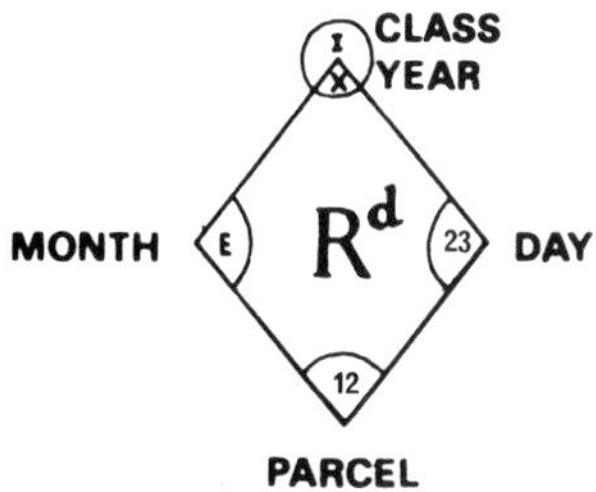

Registry mark used between 1842 and 1867. This particular one shows the date 23rd March 1842.

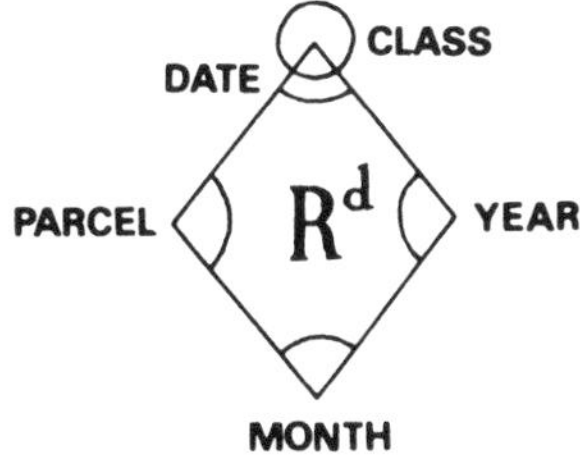

Registry mark for the years 1868–1883.

From 1884 to 1900 serial numbers were used on registered designs. The first numbers in each year were as follows: 1884 1; 1885 19754; 1886 40480; 1887 64520; 1888 90483; 1889 11648; 1890 141273; 1891 163767; 1892 185713; 1893 205240; 1894 224720; 1895 246975; 1896 268392; 1897 291241; 1898 311658; 1899 331707; 1900 351202.

The words *Trade Mark* date a piece as no earlier than 1862, *England* no earlier than 1891, with *Made in England* as a frequent 20th-century variant.

Many marks, of course, give no more than decoratively framed pattern names, but sometimes tiny initials appear here too. Really misleading marks include, for example, such pattern names as *Dresden* or *Kang-H'si.* Several firms in Victorian days, including the Mortlock china retailers, marked their wares with the 18th-century dates claimed for their establishment–and have disappointed beginner-collectors ever since.

Glass

Over two thousand years ago ancient Syrians shaped hot glass with blowpipes just as glass-blowers make some of our finest table glass today—and by then the craft of glassmaking was already another two thousand years old. Egyptian and Roman empires have left us fascinating glass relics. In Lancashire, the modern glass centre of St Helens is less than ten miles from Warrington's Roman-occupation factory.

By medieval days the Venetians were expertly fashioning this fragile soda-glass into delicate shapes brilliantly enamelled, and it was a Venetian, Verzelini, who first became successful with such delicate glassware here, as glassmaker to Elizabeth I. Little of his Anglo-Venetian work remains, however, and more collectors enjoy the substantial shapes of early English bottles in dark, workaday glass.

World renowned flint-glass

England's world renown for table glass developed only after 1674 when George Ravenscroft with a new formula evolved 'the finest and noblest glass', then called flint-glass and now usually lead crystal. This stalwart glass, heavy and shadowy with lead, suited the sturdy vessels favoured on English tables. Compared with fragile Continental soda-glass it possessed a wonderful refractive brilliance and a satisfying resonant ring.

No new collector wants overwhelming technical terms.

Briefly, a red hot gather or blob of this glass on the end of a blowing rod could be inflated by the glass-blower into the bowl of what is known as a free-blown glass. As, marvellously, glass when hot can be joined without trace, a team of glassmen could attach stem and foot to a drinking glass bowl leaving no more than a 'ponty scar' under the vessel's foot where it had been held on the end of an iron pontil rod. Heat treatment–annealing –toughened the glass (the hollow or kick under an early decanter aided this) and for strength early footrims were turned in (welted or folded). Welted feet and ponty scars long continued to be acceptable on less fashionable glass.

So much for the glassmen's terms, but what were they making by the early 18th century? Drinking glasses still had heavy bowls on thick stems and wide welted feet. The stem might be drawn as a tapering extension of the bowl sometimes enclosing an air bubble 'tear'. Or it might be 'stuck' to bowl and foot, being shaped either in a baluster outline or in the Hanoverians' (silesian) shouldered-pedestal or as a simple arrangement of swellings known as knops.

Dessert glass immediately distinguishable from a drinking glass by its decorative rim of loops and the knobs known as strawberry prunts. Its height, about 7 inches, suggests that it was intended as an orange glass, to be placed in the centre at the top of a pyramid of colourful sweetmeat glasses arranged on glass salvers. 1740s. Text page 64.

Other delights include sweetmeat glasses and custard cups arranged on glass salvers. Such stemmed salvers, two or three on top of each other and each with an array of fruits, sweets and jellies in appropriate small glasses, made colourful pyramids for the informal social gathering known as a dessert. The glasses for dry sweetmeats have ornamental rims; vessels for frothy syllabubs are wide rimmed and narrow bowled. The collector may find an early decanter in self-explanatory shaft-and-globe or mallet shape with a ball stopper; or a baluster candlestick on a high moulded foot. But by the 1740s all this was changing.

Early cut glass

Collectors welcome the early Georgian advance to lighter table glass. As the annealing process improved, design could become more delicate, and since a glass tax calculated by weight of ingredients was imposed in 1745–46 the glassmen had to make more of their materials. Many collectors think this early Georgian flint-glass table ware of the 1740s–1770s, light, small-scale and delicately ornamented, the loveliest ever made.

Delicate wheel engraving on shouldered decanters of about 1760 (magnum and quart sizes). *Left:* hop and barley motif associated with vessels for strong ale. *Right:* engraved to suggest a wine label hung on a chain around its neck. Text opposite page.

By blowing his blob of hot glass into a patterned mould before expanding it fully by further blowing, the glassman could give his vessel a gently rippled surface. But far more decisive patterns were achieved by delicately grinding shallow facets or diamond shapes into the glass–the work of a separate group of specialists, the glass cutters.

Grinding with different shapes of wheel also produced almost all the line ornament on glass. Exception to this wheel engraving was the freehand line work done with a diamond point–rare but never entirely out of use. This is sometimes a worry to the beginner who confuses such diamond point engraved decoration with diamond cutting, a term applied to the diamond-shaped patterns wheel-ground into the glass.

Examine an engraved glass closely and you can see how each flower petal down to the tiniest tendril has been cut laboriously with the fine edge of the manually revolved wheel. Wheel engraving includes delightful patterns such as the ale glass hop-and-barley. Flowered glasses suggesting ornament on the accompanying porcelain teacups were used for the potent cordials served with the evening tea. Other engraving on drinking glass bowls ranged from fruiting vines on long-stemmed champagne flutes to the cider maker's propaganda words NO EXCISE on the bucket bowls of cider glasses around 1760. Wheel engraved Jacobite glasses commemorate loyalty to the Stuart cause, mainly around 1745. These are often faked. Some decanters are magnificently engraved with names and flourished 'labels'.

Colours and gold

An obvious alternative was surface ornament painted on the glass in enamels or gold. The finest enamelling in dense white and colours is attributed to William Beilby of Newcastle and his sister Mary, at work in the 1760s–1770s–heraldic work, Rococo scrolling, even landscapes, sometimes 'signed' with a tiny butterfly (but often faked).

Gold rims have often worn off 18th-century glass, but gilded ornament is sometimes found on later 18th-century vessels. Burnished mercury gilding dates from the 1780s onwards, but glittering gold only from about 1853.

Colour in another form appeared around the mid 18th century to ornament wineglass stems. Ancient Rome delighted in this process which filled straight or swelling stems with spirals of air or white enamel or brilliant colours. The so-called mercury twist consists of thick corkscrew air spirals in especially brilliant glass. Such stems are smooth to the fingers, but some other straight stems, from the 1740s to the 1800s, were surface-incised. Others, now especially valuable, were cut all over on the grinding wheel into slightly concave finger-pleasing facets.

Table glass in clear colours was widely used from the 1750s and here gold ornament was especially effective. Flint-glass's special refractive fire was largely lost, but lovely effects were achieved in deep blues, cool watery greens and heavy reds less vermilion-bright than the imported red glass of Bohemia (Czechoslovakia). Blue, nowadays, seems always to be called Bristol blue, but in the 1760s this term was applied specifically

Bristol blue glass enriched with gold. Corresponding initial letters on the stoppers are important as each stopper was individually ground to fit a specific decanter. Text opposite page.

to a refined form of cobalt blue from Saxony. The disruption of the Seven Years War meant that for a time only one Bristol dealer could supply this magnificent colour.

Clear glass decanters were always required for wines, but the late 18th century has left many sets of spire-finialed decanters and squares for spirits in blue glass named in gold. Small blue glass bottles were gold labelled for sauces and toilet waters and delicately ornamented for scent. All the smaller table accessories may be found, too, such as finger bowls; blue glass linings perfectly displayed the perforated patterns in late 18th-century salt cellars and the like in silver or Sheffield plate.

Opaque white glass was advertised as enamel glass in the 1760s, somewhat soft surfaced and brittle but popular for jugs and sugar basins, candlesticks, finger bowls and vases, enamelled and gilded with flowers, birds and all the gay nonsense of costly contemporary porcelain. Some was transfer-printed. A poorer quality made from the 1770s onwards shows a fiery opalescence against the light, known in the 19th century as sunset glow.

Mid Georgian Neo-classicism

This cheaper white ware was a poor, low-taxed lime-soda glass, for the tax on flint-glass was doubled in 1777. Flint-glassmen then had to concentrate on high quality work, light in weight, their well-proportioned gracious designs suiting the current Neo-classical mood. Technically glass continued to improve although a merest hint of colour remained–either lacking or overdone in many fakes! This was the period of the slender decanter sloping inward or outward from shoulder to base, ornamented perhaps with wheel engraving, enamelling, gilding or shallow facet-cutting, matched on a stopper finial shaped as a spire or oval or vertical disc. Often long shallow flutes decorated the neck and lower body: in the barrel decanter shallow lines suggested hoops and staves.

Quite as important in contributing sparkle to fashionable apartments was the candlestick, elaborated into the branching candelabrum only rivalled by the spectacular hanging chandelier. Neo-classical silver prompted pillar candlestick designs on domed and terraced feet and the vase candlestick with an urn-shaped body on a square plinth. In the candelabrum gilded ormolu was combined with flashing cut glass, two or four curved branches with candle sockets extending from a sturdy central stem. Pear-shaped drops or lustres and elaborate star finials with sparkling faceted surfaces were in huge demand for candelabra and chandeliers. The period's girandole candlestick was especially charming, hung with a circle of twinkling lustres.

Drinking glasses of the 1770s–1790s are challengingly varied, the long-established wine glasses, champagne flutes and decorative small-bowled cordials being augmented, for instance, by the massive short-stemmed rummer. The huge toddy rummer appeared in the late 1780s, a purely English vessel for mixing the popular fireside drink of spiced rum and hot water. This had an ovoid bowl at first, a thick stem and a heavy square foot. By the 1800s the bowl might be bucket- or barrel-shaped, always a field for pictorial engraving. A glass pipette known as a toddy lifter was used to serve the hot rum into drinking glasses.

Dram and firing glasses were made for social occasions too. The small spirit dram of the early 18th century with little or no stem and a wide foot was developed in the second half of the century into a stumpy glass on a heavy flat disc foot intended for repeated banging on the table as 'fire', a form of acclamation. To keep sober at such celebrations toast-masters had their own deceptive-bowled glasses.

The slender flute sometimes called a ratafia glass was probably intended for the potent brandy drink known as surfeit water. But the most confusing vessel of this period is the Williamite glass sometimes called an Orange glass. The glass itself may have been made in the late 18th century, and the engraved ornament refers to William III who reigned 1689–1702. But such inscriptions are associated with end-of-century political controversy, and some date to as late as the 1820s.

Regency sparkle

Improvements in annealing meant that English flint-glass was stronger still by the end of the 18th century, prompting bolder, deeper cutting. Much glass was cut with V-shaped wheels into patterns of raised diamond points that the cutters sometimes further notched in what they called cross-cut, hobnail and strawberry patterns. Other wheels gave the glass horizontal, vertical and fan-shaped prismatic cutting or scattered it with stars and sprigs and the circular concavities known as printies. Long icicle lustres became popular, followed by flat-surfaced hanging prisms. Decanters became massive with broad rings of cut glass round their necks to make the weight easier to lift. Stoppers were vertical targets or flat mushrooms or diamond-cut spheres.

Wide-shouldered decanters belong to the early 19th century, cylindrical and the slightly tapering 'Prussian shape', some with heavy vertical reeding (convex flutes) as body ornament. Ships' decanters may be found too—and among reproductions—extremely wide based and narrow shouldered to stand steady in a gale.

Some especially heavy glass is often called Waterford, but it is a mistake to think most Irish glass is distinguishable from the

Ships' decanters, extra wide based and with four rings around the neck for easy gripping. Sometimes known as Rodney decanters. Text above.

English that it copied so well. For a time it was exempt from tax, prompting lavish, heavy pieces. But even this advantage ended in 1825 when the tax on flint-glass was 10½d per lb. A very little was marked by Belfast, Dublin and Cork glasshouses, and certain shapes seem to have been popular with Irish glassmen such as kettledrum and canoe fruit bowls. There is, too, an engraved pattern of oval and diamond lozenges formed of intersecting circles on decanters and the like that is usually known as the Cork vesica.

Among all this cut-glass glitter a special pleasure is the Apsley Pellatt crystal cameo. Here again was a notion that depended upon the perfect fusion of hot glass. A small bas relief portrait, often of royalty, was cast in china clay and completely enclosed in particularly clear flint glass. Pellatt made paperweights and other ornaments 1819–35; these were copied less perfectly around the 1850s and called medallion inlays.

Pressed glass

Brilliant geometrical deep cutting served as a background to Pellatt's silvery cameos, but cutting gradually lost favour for a time after an American process was introduced in the 1830s for pressing glass. A plunger forced the hot glass into a patterned mould, producing vessels almost as sharply ornamented on the outside as those hand-cut on the wheel. The blown-moulded process for shaping and patterning glass described on page 63 was improved early in the 19th century, but it is easy to distinguish this more gently moulded ornament, felt by the fingertips inside the vessel. In pressed glass the vessel interior is left smooth by the plunger. Dishes were pressed and mugs, bowls and tumblers. In the 1870s–1880s great use was made of stippled grounds and raised dots, for instance on commemorative plates. Opaque coloured glass is found in some cheap pressed jugs, bowls and ornaments, including marbled glass incorporating steelworks slag drawn off the molten steel at the end of the day's work–hence the name end-of-day glass. This long remained popular, and some bears the marks of North Country makers.

Nailsea pleasures

Pressed glass was a cheap follower of fashion. The glass for working folk was so-called Nailsea. From the 1790s onwards this made decorative use of much more cheaply taxed bottle glass. Simple vessels made in the murky glass were flecked and looped with white or rolled in colourful waste glass chippings. By the 1800s the glass could be cleared to a pale green, often coloured an opaque dark blue or amber.

Nailsea near Bristol was a source of superior crown glass, but gave the name to this gay bottle glass work which was made at Newcastle, Sunderland, Alloa and elsewhere. Articles ranged from jugs and conjoined gimmel flasks to such imitative nonsense as giant tobacco pipes. Stoppered rolling pins, for example, were made at first in flecked and streaked glass but later in coloured or opaque white glass which might be painted or transfer-printed with good luck verses.

For centuries, among similar working folk, spun glass caused shop front or street corner wonderment as a man or woman with a small blow lamp transformed rods of coloured glass into imaginative tiny ornaments. Doubtless some so-called friggers were spare time competitive creations, but far more of this work, such as delicately rigged ships, came late in the 19th century from small commercial ventures that also met renewed demand for glass walking sticks, bells, hunting horns and the like.

Victorian colour

The year 1845 was enormously important to English glassmen. The heavy tax on flint-glass was abolished. Now at last there was the chance to experiment in flint-glass with notions from the Continent where glass made up in colour what it lacked in sparkle. Coloured clear glass became popular, and clear glass painted in enamel colours was soon followed by more ambitious cased glass. Collectors are urged to look beyond the abundant once-cheap pinkish glass now known as cranberry. Red colouring was costly, and this is often no more than lightly tinted to hide blemishes, although here too the best was cased in preparation for deep geometrical cutting.

Cased glass is something the collector either admires or detests. Cased glass decanters were made and wine glasses, vases and toilet water bottles. Cased scent bottles included the double-ended type with a cap at each end, one still offering a whiff of aromatic smelling salts and the other perhaps a trace of a fragrant handkerchief scent.

The process consisted in covering the blown vessel of clear glass with similarly shaped layers of coloured glass often including opaque white. While hot, all perfectly fused together so that when they cooled the glass-cutter could slice through to the clear glass in slanting cuts that revealed the intervening colours in simple patterns. Flashed glass was a cheaper variant, with the glass merely dipped in colour. Staining was cheaper still, with colour applied after the vessel was completed.

Layers of clear glass were used too to enclose a silver solution or metal foil that fragmented into shimmering spangles when the glass-blower inflated the vessel. Some vessels were lightly ground to suggest frosting and some showed the metal foil through a covering of coloured glass, compared at the time to the metallic sheen of hummingbird plumage.

Brilliantly white opaque glass cased with ruby glass. This toilet water flask, $9\frac{1}{2}$ inches tall, is thought to have been made by the Bacchus firm, Birmingham. Text above. Harris Museum and Art Gallery, Preston (Mrs French collection).

Victorian glass suggesting porcelain. The tall opaline glass vase is painted with flower trails. The central vase shows Japanese influence. The jug is of clear glass closely patterned with white lines and with turquoise glass on rim and handle. Text below. Harris Museum and Art Gallery, Preston.

Collectors today value especially the period's millefiori (thousand flower) paperweights, made in England from the late 1840s. Each flower consisted of a slice cut from a slender many-coloured glass rod that had been built up, layer upon concentric layer, round a central core and then drawn out long without disturbing the pattern. When cold, slices from differently patterned rods could be arranged on a clear glass base and closely covered with a magnifying glass dome, heat ensuring perfect fusion.

Bristol dumps, high-domed door-stops in coarse green glass, came later and continued far into the 20th century, their ornament often no more than a fountain of air bubbles pricked into the hot glass.

Mid Victorians also favoured peculiarly lifeless semi-opaque opaline glass in a range of colours. Much was painted with the period's massed flowers, and figure scenes were ambitiously copied from then-popular ancient Grecian pottery. Some were coloured over transfer-printed outlines. Sometimes a plain vessel with typical rounded shaping was contrasted with relief ornament in clear coloured glass such as the period's adored reptiles. Other pieces were left plain for amateurs to do their worst.

Fancy glass

This was but one style among many offered to Victorians under the general name of fancy glass. Many of the techniques were suggested by fragile early Venetian work. But English glassmen advancing from silvered and gilded glass of the mid century could decorate more substantial flint-glass vessels ranging from popular long-necked decanters to lidded bowls for the dressing table. Slender flower vases included the épergne where the central tapering vase on a broad plateau was surrounded by scrolling arms supporting smaller vessels.

Among fancy glass the collector must seek out individual favourites from 'crackle ice' to an acid-induced satin finish. Delicate threads of coloured glass might be wound tightly around a vessel's stem or handle. Simple trails and frillings were in vogue again and sophisticated quilted effects with air bubbles trapped between layers of glass.

Skilled heating at the furnace mouth could produce a range of colours on a single vessel, as in the opaque 'Burmese' glass of the 1880s, heat-shaded from yellow to deep pink. Attractive crackled effects and greenish brownish marbling were offered in moss-agate glass, and dusky Scottish Clutha glass was introduced in heavy primitive shapes often clouded with tiny random bubbles.

The vogue for engraving

Tours de force had been shown by glass cutters at the 1851 Great Exhibition. So sharp and hostile to the fingers was their diamond patterning (to defy the makers of pressed glass) that it comes as no surprise to find mid Victorians preferring yet another alternative. This was delicate wheel engraving on clear glass. This dated back to the early 18th century and was carried into the 19th century when massive rummers displayed ships, Masonic emblems, even scenes like Wearmouth bridge and Tyne suspension bridge.

All manner of imaginative engraving in intricate revived Rococo and classical fantasy was now approved on decanters, vases in Grecian outlines, tall straight water jugs, loving cups, carafes and the newly fashionable hemispherical champagne cups. There were flowers and trailing foliage, too, of course, and feathers and the period's popular ferns. Mostly this was wheel engraving; but a little was drawn with a diamond point, and some was cheaply etched with acid.

By the 1880s deep-cut glass was in vogue again, but engravers achieved new success with a glossy style of wheel engraving. This was known at the time as rock crystal glass as it suggested the sultry beauty of carved rock crystal quartz. Some spectacular pieces were made by brilliant craftsmen and occasionally signed, and the fashion continued into the present century. Instead of being left softly opaque, the deeply engraved ornament was polished to a limpid brilliance.

Glass rummer probably made in Sunderland about 1801. The engraving shows a ship sailing under the Wearmouth Bridge, opened 1796. The reverse bears the rose, thistle and shamrock, to mark the union of Great Britain and Ireland. Text above. Victoria and Albert Museum, London.

Superb example of rock crystal glass with chinoiserie themes from the firm's collection at Royal Brierley Crystal. Late 19th century. Text page 75.

Cameo glass

In these wonder days it may be well to stress that all glass cutting and wheel engraving is individual handwork, the glass held against a revolving wheel. But some of the most difficult late Victorian work, cameo glass, now highly prized, consists of *carving* shallow bas reliefs into the cased or layered glass of a vase or other ornament. This was another ancient Roman technique, preserved in the famous Portland vase where the bas relief figures show white against the dark glass background. John Northwood, 1836–1902, was the most important English exponent and was successful too with so-called intaglio engraving where the ornament was deeply hollowed into the glass. George and Thomas Woodall carved some fine cameo glass with similar classical themes, but for commercial cameo ornament grinding wheels and acid were soon doing most of the work.

By the 1890s some semblance of this effect was achieved with thick white paint. Many so-called Mary Gregory figures painted in white on clear glass date to the 1870s–1880s. The childish antics have been widely copied ever since, often very badly and sometimes with tinted faces. This is now associated with America but mostly came from Bohemia.

Much important English glass was exported to the United States including cameo and rock crystal work. Brilliant-cut table glass was exported in huge matching suites, the ornament immensely elaborate and finely detailed. Nothing unorthodox could be expected of this status symbol work, but even here the tall attenuated outlines of end-of-century design dominated the glittering array of tall-stoppered, long-necked decanters, narrow-handled claret jugs, waisted water jugs and the champagne jugs with central ice cylinders. Even a sugar basin might have a faceted stem and star-cut foot.

Nevertheless the period has left some beautifully simple, collectable art glass by such leaders as Harry Powell of London's Whitefriars Glasshouse. Art Nouveau interest was reflected alike in slender drinking glass and writhing crimped-rim flower flute. Here cutting would have been considered a distraction from the vessel's flowing grace. At the same time late Victorian enthusiasm for Japanese art ensured a welcome for many a low squarish vessel on corner feet, some coloured and shaped to suggest carved ivory.

Important makers of 19th-century glass in Britain included among others the Powell, Bacchus, Osler and Richardson firms, Thomas Webb, Stevens & Williams and Webb & Corbett. North-east England produced much pressed glass, and Scottish glass came from the Edinburgh and Leith Glasshouse, from James Couper of Glasgow, from Dunbarton and Alloa. In France such leaders as Rousseau, Gallé and Lalique acquired international fame as they ranged far and wide among art glass techniques, as did Loetz in Austria and the Tiffany workshops in America. Like contemporary art potters, all rejoiced in technical advances aiding control of furnace heat and colour chemistry. Among Tiffany's rivals was the Englishman Frederick Carder, 1863–1963, important designer with Stevens and Williams of Stourbridge until he went to America in 1903, to retire only after another 56 years of brilliant inventive work.

Silver

More fortunate than ever today is the babe blessed with a silver christening spoon–first introduction, perhaps, to a life time of collecting minor silver far more rewarding than its ever-increasing money value. From time immemorial man has appreciated this benign metal. Many an ancient mountain silver-working testifies to the hazards he would venture for such treasure. Its gleaming brightness has complemented his beeswax candles, its purity has preserved the subtlest flavour in his cooking and it has proved clean and sweet to his lips in loving cup and wine taster.

Silver has to be hardened for normal use with a little copper. But too much of this alloy lessens its value, and silversmiths still submit their wares to quality testing and marking to conform with the ancient rules of their guild. As early as the 13th century standards of purity for silver and gold were established in London: the great Worshipful Company of Goldsmiths was incorporated in 1327. The amount of copper alloy permitted in sterling silver was defined, and a system of testing (assaying) and punch-marking was established.

Hallmarks

This system has been maintained so rigorously that anyone today handling a piece of English silver plate turns instinctively first to the row of tiny punches–hallmarks–noting the exact details of their features and also the puncheon outlines.

Accepting the fact of occasional deliberate deception, these marks aid greatly in dating a piece of silver when considered along with its general style, the way it is made, its design and ornament. When all these are 'right' the hallmarks fascinatingly fill in the details. They testify with letters and symbols to the quality of the metal (the proportion of copper alloy for sterling or for the slightly higher Britannia standard silver). They show the town where this quality was tested, together with the date, the silversmith who made it and, between 1784 and 1890, the payment of silver tax.

The would-be collector usually begins with the date letter, originally included so that faulty testing could be traced and punished. Each town used its own series of letters in different fonts and within different punch outlines, changing every St Dunstan's day (30th May). This has meant some repetition. Full

Hallmarks were such a valuable feature of a piece of silver that they were tolerated even when so clumsily applied as on this silver-gilt wine cup. The marks show the London date letter for 1616–17; the sterling mark of the lion passant gardant; the 'leopard's head' of London-marked silver; the maker's mark CB. Text above. Victoria and Albert Museum, London.

lists of London and provincial date letters in their punch outlines are essential for the serious silver collector.

Among the marks of the towns where silver was assayed, most familiar, perhaps, are London's so-called leopard's head (a full-face lion head, crowned until 1821) and, from 1773, Birmingham's anchor and Sheffield's crown. The other usual lion mark is the heraldic lion walking to the left. The head was turned full-face until 1821 when it began to look straight ahead. This mark indicates silver of sterling quality. Around the end of the 17th century sterling silver was in short supply even for coin, so silversmiths had to fashion their table wares from a different quality of silver which was purer and less sturdy. The marks for this were a figure of Britannia and a lion's head with a wavy neckline ('erased'). This Britannia or high standard silver and its marks have been in minor use ever since.

Yet another date guide is the monarch's head, showing the maker's payment of tax between December 1784 and 1890. Doubled tax in 1797–98 meant two impressions of George III's head on that year's silver. Often makers, too, can be identified. Makers' marks lost their early symbols in favour of initials, except on Britannia standard silver where the law required the first two letters of the surname.

Other occasional marks include the thistle on some Scottish sterling silver from 1750 and the Irish crowned harp. Unfortunately many articles were exempted from marking from 1739, including filigree work, very rich ornament and much that weighed less than ten pennyweight (less than five pennyweight from 1790).

Early domestic silver

Silver marks, of course, are no more than a necessary preliminary to the fascinating study of silver plate itself. This must usually begin in a museum or among the treasures (frequently gilded) in ancient city or college hall. Domestic silver offers a wonderful commentary on social history because intended primarily for use, but this has meant scant respect for outmoded design. The wonder is that so much remains from Tudor and early Stuart days. Spoons, for example, are still found with the period's straight stems ending in ornamental knops such as acorn, seal, heraldic lion and widely reproduced maidenhead and apostle figure. Grander pieces include the standing salt and loving cup, ceremonial symbols in early feasting, and silver-mounted drinking horns, mazer bowls and coconut cups.

The well-to-do Tudor or Stuart schoolboy was provided with his own silver beaker and spoon, and the fastidious traveller relied on his set of nesting cups fitted with a folding spoon and knife and the fork that gradually crept into 17th-century fashion. These early drinking vessels were 'raised'; the silversmith rounded his vessel from the flat silver entirely by prolonged hammering, with frequent heating to keep the metal workable. Ornament included engraved lines, deep embossing hammered from behind (repoussé), and flatter work with small hammered punches (chasing). In the shallow saucer vessel used by the wine taster the embossed pattern aided scrutiny of the wine; the period's sturdy tankard illustrated another style of ornament in the casting that served as the lid thumbpiece.

Silver tankard showing the characteristic features of the mid 17th century. Made by Anthony Ficketts and hallmarked in London in 1650. Text above.

Post-Restoration glitter

Silver in pleasantly restrained design met varied needs in the wealthy early 17th-century household including many an attractive covered cup, the pair of handles cast perhaps as caryatids, the lid shaped so that it could be inverted as a shallow dish on a stemmed foot. But a new era of silversmithing started when Charles II and his court returned from Holland in 1660 with new ideas of domestic comfort. Among the more extravagant glitter, such as elaborate gilded silver toilet sets, the collector notes sturdy pillar candlesticks on square bases and early vessels for coffee, tea and chocolate (the latter distinguished by a small lid aperture for stirring with a swizzle stick). Among spoons there was a change to arching stems and notched, forward-curving ends.

The phrase William-and-Mary silver usually implies the important 1690s–1700s period happily associated with much charming domestic silver from the upright snuffer stand to the notch-rimmed monteith bowl for cooling wine glasses. Much silver was decorated merely with rims of the repetitive light-

Light-catching gadroon ornament on a silver candlestick. London hallmark for 1691. Text opposite page.

catching knuckles known as gadrooning, with embossed and chased acanthus leaf borders and cast finials such as flames and crouching lions. Plain-bodied sugar and pepper casters were never more delightfully perforated. But more adventurous designs and ornament came at this time with the arrival of Huguenot refugees suggesting new ways to strengthen the softer, purer silver that the smith had to use between 1697 and 1720.

The real Queen Anne silver

Looking back it is easy to see how the flamboyant late 17th century's somewhat heavy Baroque silver design was transformed into the gracious style of real Queen Anne silver. Anne reigned only 1702–14 but is associated with silver design through the first twenty years of the 18th century. This is further confused by a Victorian tendency to give her name to much of their own silver.

There is a simple shapeliness about the real Queen Anne silver, in well-balanced baluster outlines with high domed lids and curving swan-neck spouts. Even in minor items such as candlestick and caster the baluster or pear-shape prevailed, the plain surfaces enriched with the English silversmith's renowned engraving.

At this period the tea-making ritual was served by a particularly charming tea equipage. Water in a silver kettle was kept boiling on its stand over a lamp. The hostess unlocked her silver canister and made tea for each of her guests in a tiny teapot with lidded spout. The cream ewer for cold milk only gradually replaced the hot milk pot, but a covered silver sugar bowl was usual and slender tongs for the lumps chipped off the sugar-loaf as well as silver spoons in their spoon dish. Perfect finishing touch was a spoon-shaped mote skimmer, its pierced bowl skimming dust from the poured tea and its barbed end clearing the huge leaves of china tea from inside the teapot spout.

As already mentioned special hallmarks tell collectors when they encounter articles made in the soft cool-toned Britannia standard silver compulsory for silversmiths at this time. These had to be designed with especial skill. Ewers, tankards, covered cups, even casters and coffee pots might be encircled with strengthening bands, often twinkling with gadroons. But a more imaginative development was the vertical corrugation of melon fluting that shapes the rounded body of many a kettle and teapot. Possible weakness where spout or handle was attached to a vessel's curving body was met by the decorative ornament known as cut-card work. A thin piece of silver cut in formal or foliate pattern was attached to the surface around the joint.

Early Georgian elegance

When silversmiths could use sterling silver once more they worked it boldly, with a new confidence. Strong square outlines and substantial mouldings characterise such typical pieces of the 1720s–1730s as the rectangular tea canister with high-stepped lid, the popular small tray known as a waiter, the trencher salt with incurving sides and clipped concave corners. This clipped-corner outline was an alternative to the octagonal shaping that then gave character to the baluster outlines in every kind of silverware from tea-table taperstick to the handle of the silver bell gracing the tray of the period's inkstand. The other alternative was the sphere, for 'bullet' tea kettle, sugar bowl and straight-spouted teapot.

Rococo and chinoiserie

Such forthright early Georgian design ensured a welcome for the contrasting style of amusing extravaganza, French-inspired, that later centuries have dubbed Rococo. Because silversmithing is primarily concerned with shapely practical wares for those with an eye–and a purse–for sophisticated elegance, this Rococo mood was particularly attractive, gay without absurdity. Pleasure in ornament exquisitely chased was expressed in a wealth of scrolls and flowers and curving shells, in flowing asymmetrical patterns. Sometimes the design contained cherubs or seahorses or romantic Gothic pillars, sometimes swirling

Rococo gaiety of scrolls, shells and chinoiseries on a set of silver tea canisters. Made by J. Holland and London hallmarked for 1762. Text below.

flames. Especially popular were Chinamen, pagodas and all the European notions of Chinese ornament now termed chinoiserie. This was minutely detailed on jaunty little salt cellars, for instance, and sets of tea canisters.

In tea ware this happy riot of ornament appeared on teapots and kettles in inverted pear outline with fantastic spouts and on many a supremely collectable cream jug, three footed, with tip-tilted handle and spout. Small trays or salvers became increasingly important, often with rims extravagantly cast and chased. In early Georgian days even the tankard acquired a swelling tulip shape on a moulded footring, with a double-dome lid and a double-scroll handle.

Paul de Lamerie, at work in London 1711–51, is famous for Rococo fantasy. He was so skilled in working the fine Britannia standard silver that he continued with it into the 1730s. Like Pierre Harache and Augustin Courtauld, he was of Huguenot descent.

Adam Neo-classical grace

Much early Georgian silver was comparatively plain, of course, to meet domestic needs. But such work made the most of forceful baluster outlines, boldly curving spouts and handles, ornate feet on jug and salt cellar and gravy boat. Reaction from all this extravagance was the more emphatic in consequence when, soon after the mid 18th century, fashion gave its renewed approval to classical antiquity.

More and more young men of fashion were touring Europe and could glimpse for themselves the wonders of classical civilisation, and it was easy for such influential leaders of fashion as architect Robert Adam to win overwhelming approval for his Neo-classic ideals. These, it must be stressed, were far from the solemn pomp of earlier and later classical revivals. Adam himself, who included silver among his designs for interior furnishings, wrote of novelty, variety and amusement. With his sphinxes and rams' heads, his bows and flower swags, he shared his pleasure in a light-hearted romantic adaptation of classical design and ornament that in lesser hands tended to become somewhat stereotyped.

In shape all was curving grace. Tall slender-footed pots for tea and coffee were given graceful urn outlines with high-shouldered handles and tapering spouts. Lidded jugs might be in amphora outline on tripod bases, favoured, too, for ornate candelabra; candlesticks were square-based classical columns.

Workaday silver reflected such glories in simple graceful outlines and a range of obvious Neo-classical ornaments, immediately comparable with the Wedgwood ceramics then widely fashionable. Silversmiths had to meet demands of customers in increasing numbers who were new to such pleasures of gracious living and welcomed cheaper silver-substitutes. To compete, many evolved factory methods of shaping and assembling their silver: hence modifications of Neo-classical design to accept, for example, straight-sided teapots and caddies, often oval on plan. The collector has only to compare perforated work such as the 18th century's lovely baskets to see the saving in labour when regular die-stamping took over from the delicate hand piercing detectable by minute discrepancies in detail.

Characteristic features of the 1780s–1790s include the shallow fluting and convex reeding that strengthened thin, price-trimmed silverware. In contrast a considerable weight of silver was clearly indicated by the use of another fashionable form of ornament, known as bright-cutting. At a period when table glass was beginning to sparkle with deep diamond-cutting the

Bright-cut engraving on teaspoons in the simple outlines typical of the 1770s–90s. These bear the mark of the firm run by Hester Bateman, which is not to suggest that they were her personal work. Text below.

silversmith used specially shaped gouges to cut away tiny facets of the metal and burnish the resultant hollows.

The famous firm run by Hester Bateman (widowed 1760, *d.* 1794) is associated with some of this work, but is perhaps over-praised. Her workshops produced pleasant, medium quality work, including spoons which by then had gracefully arching stems and smoothly rounded ends, some in the waisted fiddle outline. Sets of the late 18th century's slender silver teaspoons, almost exactly matching and with bright-cut ornament, delight many a cautious collector.

Matthew Boulton, 1728–1809, was a progressive silversmith remembered also for silver's great rival, Sheffield plate. This English invention (in Sheffield, 1742) meant that silver wares could be imitated more cheaply in silver fused upon copper (see Chapter 6).

Regency magnificence

One answer to such unwelcome competition came from master silversmiths making immensely rich, magnificent silver vases, urns, candelabra, wine coolers and tureens in the massive style of Neo-classicism associated with the years around the Regency (1811–20). This new enthusiasm for classical design was fostered by much serious work on discoveries at Herculaneum and Pompeii and in Egypt. Silversmiths' designers and patrons revelled in Imperial Roman grandeur and exotic Egyptian symbolism. Especially important was the silversmith Paul Storr, at work 1792–1821. His superb craftsmanship is seen in many ceremonial vessels with sculptural figures and animal supports on massive pedestals loaded with weighty castings, every detail perfectly worked.

Today, however, the collector of Regency silver may well be attracted by an entirely different range of articles. Teapots by then were matched into sets with milk and sugar vessels and were never more pleasing. The pot itself was often almost plain in a low, squat shape with a short spout and an upswept cape around the lid opening.

For really tiny treasures the collector looks for vinaigrettes, the decoratively lidded boxes filled with sponge soaked in refreshing aromatic vinegar, small enough for the daintiest reticule. Characteristically, early examples tend to look small and plain compared with later, more imaginative work, but these have the most exquisite perforated patterns in their inner gilded lids. And there are tea caddy spoons and ladles in such shapes as tealeaves, shells and scoops. Some collectors search

Silver vinaigrette, the outer lid opened to show the gilded perforated grill that secured the fragment of sponge soaked in aromatic vinegar. Text above.

out small pocket graters, still perhaps carrying fragments of nutmeg for spicing a glass of wine.

By the 1830s and 1840s silver was expected to declare its value in florid embossing and casting, most especially of flower and leaf, shell and scroll that somehow lacked the vivacity of the previous mid century's Rococo. Fat little bacchantes in high relief scrambled among fruiting vines on the wine coasters that served as stands for cut glass decanters and on the tickets naming the liquors that hung on chains round the decanters' necks. These wine labels, too, are eagerly collected. But again the collector finds particularly interesting silver for more personal use such as snuffboxes for table and pocket illustrating every kind of silver ornament. Many, like the slim cases carried by afternoon callers for their visiting cards, are pleasingly textured with the formal line patterning known as engine turning.

Imaginative Victorians

Early Victorians combatted the growing ugliness of their surroundings with wildly romantic home furnishings. Form may often appear to us deplorable, overweighty towards the base like the crinolined lady and rendered grotesque by over-size feet. But the ornament is rich in imaginative story-telling details and even little scenes. Most ambitious was presentation silver, such as plateaux and épergnes for the table centre and caskets and inkstands for the library desk.

Elaborate silver sculptures with people, animals and ornate buildings rising from naturalistic vegetation were displayed at the 1851 Great Exhibition and were considered appropriate reward whether for civic dignitary or champion racehorse owner. Impossible to polish, these doubtless prompted the period's approval of contrasting frosted and burnished surfaces.

Among useful silver, sometimes every part of a teapot's surface was embossed and chased with picture detail (Teniers was a long favoured source and Moorish scenes had a mid century vogue). Lid finial, spout and feet were figure castings. Ornament of flowers, insects and birds in high relief prompted the mid century vogue for such items as tea sets (for tea and coffee, cream and sugar), condiment sets, spoons, inkstands and chamber candlesticks shaped as flowers, shells and the like. Popular hard-wearing melon shaping is particularly attractive. By the 1850s even such long-cherished naturalism as the vine-wreathed claret jug was a trifle outmoded, perhaps, but proved as enduring as Victorian 'Elizabethan' borders of interlaced strapwork and oval cartouches.

Victorian silver testifies to the fact that its makers were marvellous craftsmen but worked to the orders of professional designers lacking practical knowledge of techniques. Behind them again stood the customer, and the many critics of the period had no hesitation in calling his taste deplorable! Attempts to improve it were led by the Society of Arts including especially Sir Henry Cole whose Felix Summerly Art Manufactures produced in a wide range of materials from 1846 attempted, albeit briefly, to associate 'the best art with familiar objects in every-day use'.

One result was the decade's delight in appropriate ornament laboriously indicating its purpose, at a time when exact replicas in silver or other metal could be made mechanically. These electrotypes are described in the following chapter.

Rival electroplate

If this association of artists and craftsmen was important to the silversmith it became infinitely more urgent when a new range of customers, inexperienced, uninhibited, discovered the glittering splendour of silver ware in far cheaper electroplated silver. This too is considered in the following chapter, but it is as well here to understand these confusing terms. Articles made of sterling and Britannia standard silver are spoken of as *silver plate*. But *Sheffield plate* has its sterling silver surfaces fused to a core of copper. *Plated silver* or *electroplate* as patented by the Elkington Company in 1840 is ware wholly constructed of a cheaper nickel alloy which is finally masked by a thin coating of pure silver deposited by an electrical process.

For innumerable middling families this electroplate meant that delicately flavoured foods could be enjoyed long before stainless steel tablewares became available. For the collector it means that high Victorian design is encountered in far greater quantity. Electrotypes spread exact knowledge of classical forms and decoration, and through the 1860s and 1870s almost every fashionable silver coffee pot and claret jug, for example, had to be a long-necked version of a Greek vase.

At this period contrast might be introduced by parcel (part) gilding and oxidising might give the silver a range of tints from white to black. Much traditional work from inkstand to grape scissors consisted of assemblies of lavish castings, condemned by such influential writers as Owen Jones who urged flat, stylised pattern.

Characteristic Gothic ornament and lettering too persisted

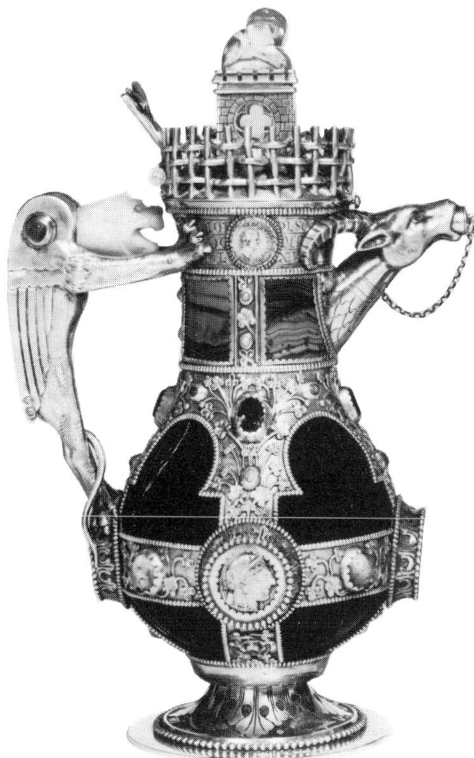

Fantastic silver designs by William Burges. The silver-mounted glass bottle is set with semi-precious stones and Greek and Roman coins. The drinking cup is set with stones and enamelled. Dated 1865–6 and 1863. Text page 92. Victoria and Albert Museum, London.

through later Victorian days and far into Edward VII's reign for church and ceremonial plate. But the depression of the late 1870s hastened a general return to lighter design, stamped and pierced in fragile imitations of Neo-classicism with Adam and Regency features to confuse the unwary collector.

Leading commercial firms offered the well-to-do such sumptuous wares as Mappin & Webb's 'Cellini' and 'Louis XVI' tea services. But among simpler workaday table pieces the collector may find, for example, silver frames to hold sauce bottles, cruets and increasingly ingenious arrangements of eggcups and gilt-bowled eggspoons.

Lively 'medieval' designs were produced by such artists as William Burges, 1827–81, and the romantic-medieval idea of designer-craftsman guilds for makers of silver ware was an important outcome of the Arts and Crafts enthusiasm stimulated by William Morris and his associates.

Arts and Crafts

The turn of the century was an exciting period for craft schools and individual talent among those who admired silver for its intrinsic flowing grace, the grey sheen of hand-hammered surfaces and patterns of delicate wire and cable twists. Some tall Art Nouveau shapes were approved with curving plant ornament, but tended to be less extravagant than Continental design. For colour the purists favoured the satisfying richness of enamels and roundly shaped cabochon stones and Baroque pearls, away from the costly glitter of faceted jewels. Some, such as Gilbert Marks, insisted on handwork; the most notable C. R. Ashbee at his Guild and School of Handicraft sought a compromise between hand and machine processes but was priced out of business by 1909.

At the other extreme the remarkable 'modern' Victorian Christopher Dresser, 1834–1904, and a minority of fellow professional designers for leading silversmiths introduced coldly angular, functional forms, machine-produced from a minimum of factory-prepared material.

Often recognised at a glance today is the silver commissioned and sold by the Liberty firm. Japanese design had an important Influence on all art work of this period, but this Liberty silver reflected current appreciation of the Celtic mood. It was made in Birmingham from 1900 and sold as Liberty's Cymric silver. It suggested hand-hammered Arts and Crafts work, but costs were cut by use of the purists' least-admired machine processes such as spinning and die-stamping.

Far more late Victorian and early Edwardian commercial silver, however, was still cast and stamped into confusions of 18th-century styles and unhelpfully called Rococo or Queen Anne. Much thin silver tea ware was strengthened on the lower part of the body with close vertical reeding. Tea caddies and the like, heavily embossed with all-over flower patterning, were safely termed 'old English'.

Clock in Liberty's Cymric silver design of an Egyptian pylon with the period's wide top and base in production throughout the Edwardian period. 1900. Text above.

Sheffield Plate

Copper coins minted in Roman London may still glimmer with traces of a silver coating. So great is silver's appeal that through subsequent centuries men tried many ways of applying the precious metal over iron, steel, copper and base metal alloys. This might aim to suggest the beautiful craftwork of the silversmith; but, at a strictly practical level, harness might be protected from rust or urn taps from corrosion, and the fastidious diner's table cutlery was made safe from tainting the subtle flavours of fruit or fish.

The ancient idea of wrapping the base metal in layer upon layer of thinly beaten silver leaf eventually became practical in the process known as French plating. Late in the 18th century this was improved as close plating and became important in Sheffield and Birmingham from about 1805. Silver rolled to a filmy-thin foil was skilfully applied with a trace of tin and great heat and pressure to cutlery, candle snuffers and the like.

More conspicuously, from 1840, articles constructed in base metals could be covered completely with silver by the process known as electroplating. But for almost exactly a century, from the 1740s to the 1840s, the magnificent answer to the age-long yearning for less costly silver table wares was Sheffield plate. This wholly English notion was unique and for a period was so successful that Sheffield was setting the fashion for far more costly work in solid silver.

Sheffield plate (and closely associated Roberts plate and British plate) totally differed from other silvered metal wares because here the silvering process came first, before manufacture. A thin layer of silver was fused by heat to a thicker layer of cheaper copper while both metals were still brick-like ingots.

Early coffee pot made from single-sided Sheffield plate. The lid and foot (where both sides might be in view) were made by placing two pieces of the single-sided fused plate together, copper to copper, with the upper layer of silver turned over to conceal the copper edges. About 1760. Text page 96. Sheffield City Museum.

Rolling into flat sheets still left the copper evenly covered with its proportionately thinner layer of sterling silver. For the first time the great status symbol of silver brilliance in ornament and table wares could be paraded in innumerable middle class homes. For years it would be virtually indistinguishable from silver plate.

The new techniques

It is the delight of collectors today to discover the small differences and so identify Sheffield plate. But at the time only the makers knew just how different and how much more difficult it was at every stage of manufacture, to raise and seam, to pierce and chase and engrave this far cheaper fused plate.

The process originated with Thomas Bolsover (his spelling of his name, though some spell it Boulsover) 1704–88, of Sheffield. He began in 1742 by making buttons and advanced no further than such small wares as snuffboxes and buckles. It was left to his former apprentice Joseph Hancock to extend the range of technique and products.

Like moulded glass and pinchbeck jewellery and the 18th century's other gay pretences, Sheffield plate was successful because it was comparatively cheap. In 1784 when the silversmith's costs were increased by a tax of sixpence an ounce (one shilling and sixpence by 1815) Sheffield plate could be sold at one-third his prices. But what problems it entailed. At first the silver covered the copper on only one side. Hollow ware was tinned inside, and some articles were made from two sheets of Sheffield plate placed back to back.

From about 1765 it was usual to fuse an ingot of silver to each face of the copper. But even then every article, from ornate épergne to simple tankard, still required a mask of silver on every cut edge where the copper showed as a raw red line. Using the silversmith's techniques the manufacturer 'raised' his bowls and saucers by long hammering and annealing and shaped their edges inch by inch in a steel-jawed swage; much care was needed not to damage the delicate silver surface.

Final burnishing and polishing had to leave the ware impeccably smooth and bright. But those raw copper edges long proved a special problem. They soon revealed the underlying colour when early Sheffield plate men merely turned them over or masked them with silver solder.

The solution to this problem really decided the success of Sheffield plate. At first the platers thought they had found it when George Whateley patented Sheffield plate wire, an astonishing small achievement. For centuries men had made silver wire by drawing it out gradually from an inch-thick rod. Now they found that fused copper and silver could produce copper wire entirely encased in silver, and this could be flattened into ribbon without revealing its red core.

Early wares

When by the 1780s this too proved vulnerable as an edging the platers used costlier solid silver wire. But by then Sheffield plate was securely established as part of the English Neo-classical scene. Candlesticks, for instance, were never more splendid than in the 1770s when Sheffield designers forged ahead of tradition-bound silversmiths. Many a handsome specimen remains, its Corinthian column rising from a square plinth.

By the 1780s a shouldered tapering pillar might be topped by an urn candle socket with ornament on all parts in deep relief. The candelabrum was especially impressive, its central socket supporting two or more arms scrolling or twisting around a central finial.

For pipe-lighting and letter-sealing the Sheffield plate wax-jack offered an open stand supporting a spool and waxpan for a coil of flexible wax taper held in a metal clip, giving a glimmer of light that burnt out safely if forgotten. Another interesting item introduced as early as the 1770s was the gravy argyle, suggesting a teapot with a low-set, excessively slender spout. Inside, either a hot water compartment or a central box iron ensured that guests could serve themselves to the best of the gravy piping hot.

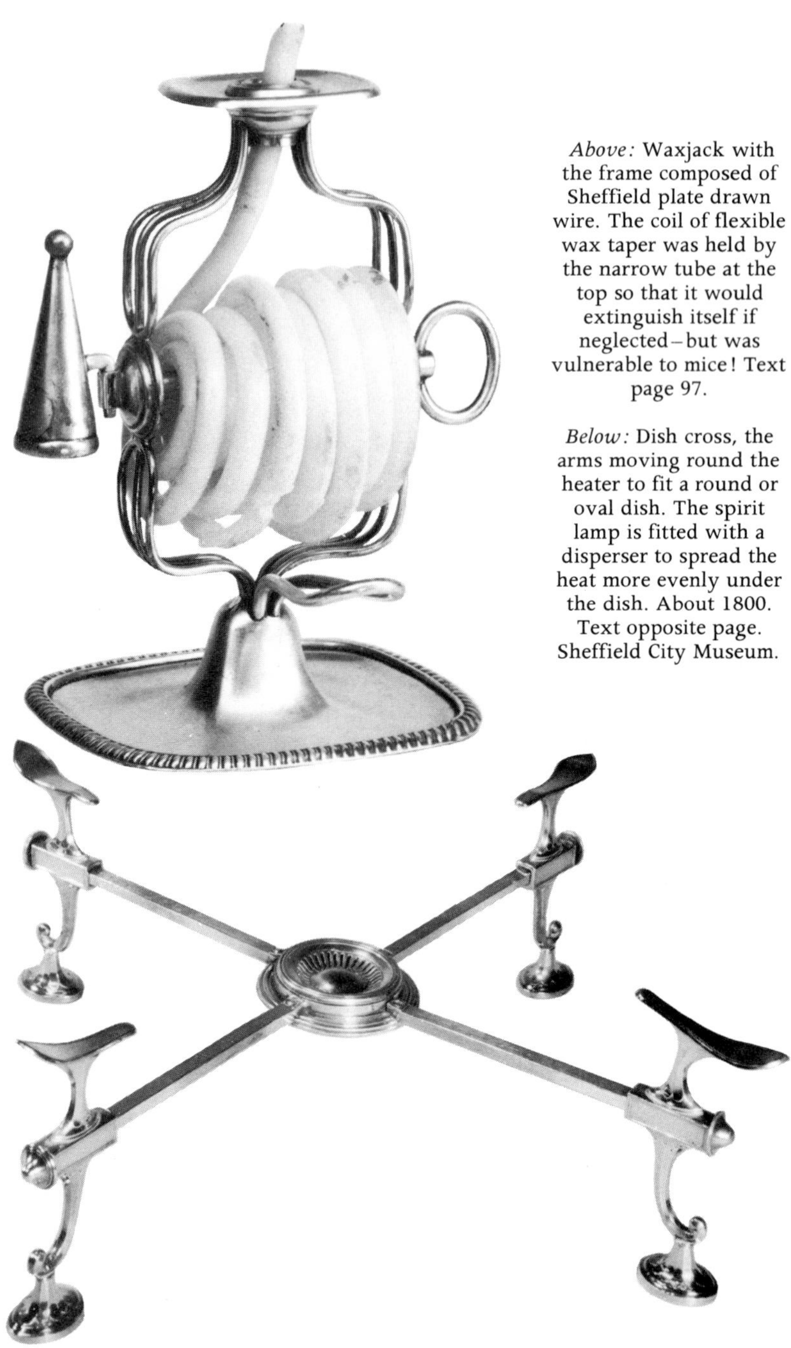

Above: Waxjack with the frame composed of Sheffield plate drawn wire. The coil of flexible wax taper was held by the narrow tube at the top so that it would extinguish itself if neglected – but was vulnerable to mice! Text page 97.

Below: Dish cross, the arms moving round the heater to fit a round or oval dish. The spirit lamp is fitted with a disperser to spread the heat more evenly under the dish. About 1800. Text opposite page. Sheffield City Museum.

The box iron was long favoured for heating magnificent Sheffield plate urns (see page 121), but for hot serving dishes another early Sheffield plate suggestion was the dish cross. This had four horizontal pivoting arms radiating from a central spirit lamp. Each arm was fitted with a bracket linked to a small foot and these could be moved along the arms to hold any size of dish rim.

Marks

Early Sheffield plate seldom offers the collector any helpful marks. As early as 1773 silversmiths felt their ware sufficiently threatened to have a law passed that banned marks of any kind on its upstart rival. When marks were permitted, from 1784, they had to include the maker's name in full. Since these could never resemble silver hallmarks few makers registered or used them.

Any marks found on Sheffield plate are most likely to indicate Victorian work. Superficially similar British plate from 1836 was often marked with unregistered devices much like silver hallmarks. Occasionally too a collector finds a crown mark to distinguish Sheffield plate from poor quality Continental work imported after 1815.

I have stressed already that the lower cost of the material made Sheffield plate profitable and encouraged manufacturers to devise elaborate ways of overcoming its problems. Ornament especially prompted factory methods more efficient than much traditional silversmithing.

The problems of ornament

Always with Sheffield plate the main concern was to avoid breaking or bruising or cutting through the thin silver surface and revealing the copper. This ruled out at once all normal engraving. Instead, some patterns were flat-chased with small punches expertly tapped. But even for much of such low relief work and for all high relief or repoussé ornament the Sheffield plate men soon found it best to press the fused metal with stamping hammers into dies cut in blocks of cast steel. The steel was hardened after being hollowed into delicately detailed patterns. For example the stem of a pillar candlestick could be decorated all over in relief before being curled into a tube and vertically seamed.

Obviously silversmiths made it as hard as possible for Sheffield plate to imitate their fashionable patterns: by the 1780s, when extraordinarily clear-cut Sheffield plate ornament was die-stamped in high relief, the silversmiths turned to the scintillating sharp-angled engraving known as bright cutting. But even this was closely simulated with die-stamping and chasing.

Some engraving on Sheffield plate was inescapable–family crests and the like. In early work an article such as a salver might have a hole cut and filled with a piece of silver where the engraving would come. Soon the silver was merely soldered over the surface, and eventually it was found that a circle or rectangle of pure silver could be 'rubbed in' until it seemed to become part of the surface (easily detected when tarnished, for only pure silver would adhere, and the silver of Sheffield plate is sterling standard).

Sometimes a pinprick can be seen marking the centre of such an area. This would serve as a guide to the engraver, who would probably be a specialist employed by the shop selling the ware.

Perforated pattern was another problem, which may be why Georgian silversmiths delighted in pierced cake baskets, dish rings and decanter coasters. In many vessels such as sugar and cream pails the piercing made a decorative feature of the blue glass linings. Nevertheless, despite the prospect of all those tiny red edges, the Sheffield plate men produced all these charming items too and many more. They could not use the silversmith's newly developed piercing saw, but another tool was devised–a fly-punch consisting of a piercing tool and a steel bed that exactly fitted it. Hole by hole the sheet of Sheffield plate was pierced before assembly, the tool dragging down the silver over the sides of the perforation.

The later 1780s and 1790s were wonderful years for superb Sheffield plate, marred only by the effect of war upon the export market. From about 1785, when solid silver satisfactorily masked the edges, makers could indulge to the full in splendidly ambitious ornamental designs. Among the most elaborate was the épergne or table centre which originated in silver for offering sauces and spices. An open frame on four scrolling legs supported a central table dish, while around it rose curved branches carrying smaller dishes similarly chased and pierced. These might be filled with fruits or sweetmeats; sometimes, if required, they could be exchanged for candle sockets.

Wirework

In an early épergne even the handles of the small basket dishes

Cake basket constructed from Sheffield plate wires, hairpin-shaped and soldered to rim and base, a style fashionable from about 1790. Text page 102.

would be punch-perforated hole by hole. But an obvious alternative was to construct the basket–or toast-rack or cruet stand or many another lightweight article–entirely in Sheffield plate wire. This was set off by a lining of rich blue glass. The wire, rolled into flat ribbon, was ideal for the small basket handles and for sugar tongs and other little details where soldered-on edges would be clumsy. Wiremaking was improved about 1780 and perfected in 1800.

At first a vessel might be composed of short U-shaped wires fixed between rim and base by drilled holes and solder; early in the 19th century came S-shaped wires, followed by a continuous wire pattern–and followed too by less perfectly soldered modern imitations.

Sheffield plate like silver in the years around the end of the century showed many contrasts between this lightweight work and such substantial pieces as tea and coffee sets including hot water, cream and sugar vessels arranged on ornate tea trays. The late 18th century's severe straight-sided teapots gave place to the extremely attractive low-bodied oval with a flaring collar around the lid opening. But this lively shape all too soon expanded into a drooping outline.

Teapot with the caped effect around the lid typical of the 1800s, matched by sugar bowl and jug. Made by George Ashforth and Company. Text above.

For the connoisseur's coffee the period's vessel was the squat, straight-sided lamp-supported coffee biggin, fitted inside with a fabric filter like a small child's biggin cap. But most handsome of all was the urn (and remember that the guests would view the imposing 'classical' outline with the clumsy tap hidden at the back). The wide bowl shape was never bettered and suited the period's heavy reeding or gadrooning on lid, body and ball-footed plinth.

From about 1790 lavish ornament on such a piece might include decorative silver mounts such as scrolls and shells. Sheffield plate could not be cast, of course, so it came naturally to these manufacturers to die-shape such mounts far more cheaply from thin silver and weight them with molten solder.

Late Georgian contrasts

Many a guest seeing such gleaming ornament on tea tray or wine cooler must have been persuaded that the ware was costly silver through and through. Indeed the Sheffield plate men were so alert to this enjoyment of harmless deception that they might fit an ornate egg-cup stand with egg-cups (that the breakfast guest could scrutinise closely) made of hallmarked silver. Master silversmiths encouraged this pompous wealth-flaunting attitude to weighty silver, but it was of little real service to the Sheffield plate manufacturer, despite many an ornate inkstand loaded with silver mounts. His table candlesticks, for example, lost their fine Neo-classical grace in favour of massive ornament on socket, shoulder and heavily weighted base. An ingenious design here is the straight, squat-looking stick not always recognised as telescopic, able to double its height.

One trouble for the Sheffield plate manufacturer was the high cost of the elaborate dies that shaped the fused metal. It was dangerously tempting to continue outmoded patterns. One way of cutting costs, however, was to follow another method long practised by factory silversmiths and shape hollow ware by spinning. By the 1820s copper was available that was pliant enough for a flat sheet of Sheffield plate to be revolved on a lathe against a wooden form that gradually forced it into the required bowl or other hollow ware. The collector looks for tiny spiralling lines inside the vessel.

Practical table wares

Spun work, thin and vulnerable, is despised by some collectors. But at least this period's price-cutting thin plate prompted such appealing dent-withstanding designs as melon shaping, fluting and reeding. The great range of styles and qualities in Regency and late Georgian plate can only be realised by examining a major collection such as the display in Sheffield City Museum.

Designers must have been as confused as collectors may be today by the renewed interest in contrasting Greek and Rococo shapes and increasing demand for laboriously naturalistic detail. But such a collection indicates too how much plain Sheffield plate was made for practical everyday service. Sumptuous tureens and ornate wine coolers, for example, may be easier to find today than homely hard-worked egg boilers, toast-racks and similar aids to fine breakfasts and suppers.

The cheese toaster was a practical notion. This is a shallow rectangular dish containing half a dozen individual pans over a hot water compartment. A handle at the back enables it to be thrust towards the fire, the hand being protected by a hinged lid held half open by a chain. The lid perfectly reflects the fire's heat on to rounds of toast piled with cheese that thus can be browned while flat in their small pans.

A tube-and-blade device for slicing fresh cucumber at table is another intriguing Sheffield Museum exhibit. Self-service was offered too by the Sheffield plate tea-and-coffee machine. This consists of an urn mounted over a spirit lamp that swivels to replenish either of two smaller urns, all grouped on a stand with a basin for unwanted dregs.

One of these machines in Sheffield Museum has the name and churchwarden pipe mark used by Daniel Holy, Wilkinson & Co. Such a mark is an unexpected bonus, although a quality mark is sometimes noted such as the *SILVER EDGES* used by Matthew

Typical of many a matching set, this egg stand includes salt cellar and four eggcups all gilded inside and four eggspoons gilded all over. Made by A. Goodman and Company about 1805. Text opposite page. Sheffield City Museum.

Boulton. A few firms indicated the proportion of silver to copper, which by the end of the 18th century was about 1 to 15 and soon became lower still.

The arrival of 'nickel silver'

By the 1840s hard-hit Sheffield plate makers might skimp their silver until it was down to a proportion of 1 to 50. But by then manufacture had nearly ceased. The first challenge came from Roberts plate in 1830. A whitish alloy of copper, zinc and nickel, known as nickel silver but containing no silver, was introduced between silver and copper. Tough British plate followed in 1836 with the nickel silver replacing the copper. All the familiar Sheffield plate items were made by the old methods, easily recognised where the rub of wear shows a cold yellowish grey metal instead of mellow copper.

The real change came in 1840 when several men's far-sighted experiments culminated in a patent taken out by the Elkington firm for what we know as electroplate. Articles were constructed in nickel silver, and an electrical deposit process covered them with minute particles of pure silver. This silver frosting had to be scratch-brushed and polished into a faultless surface.

The process was improved, making the power-driven polishing less arduous, but the essential difference remained. In Sheffield plate, sterling silver was fused by heat upon copper before manufacturing processes began. In electroplate, pure silver was added last, so that it masked all constructional detail. The letters *EPNS* often mark such plate (*E*lectro *P*lated *N*ickel *S*ilver).

Early Victorians adored presentation trophies and table ornaments fashioned as factual three-dimensional scenes. By

Cheese toaster shown in the working position. Made by Matthew Boulton, Birmingham, about 1800. Text page 104. Sheffield City Museum.

Elkington's electrical processes the most elaborate ornamental figure could be copied exactly in every detail in the nickel alloy and then electroplated in pure silver. At the Great Exhibition of 1851 electroplating was hailed for its ornamental possibilities in both silver and gold rather than for the inexpensive table elegance that we think of today. (For tarnish-free surfaces of gold it avoided the appalling health hazards to the workers involved in gilding with mercury.)

A mechanical copy, known as an electrotype or galvano, could be built up by the electrodeposit process as a replica of any item, even of a precious ancient classical ornament, which would be copied first (from moulds) in wax or composition. But Elkington price lists, issued between 1855 and 1862, already showed a huge range of table wares.

Styled 'rich Elizabethan', 'Arabesque' and the like, this electroplate ranged from a seven-guinea claret jug to fiddle pattern teaspoons at 16 shillings a dozen. Table forks very strongly plated and with silver points were £3 5s a dozen–and more for ornate patterns. Teapots were offered in all the styles of their day from low cushion shapes to the tall straight-sided vessel with melon swellings or vaguely Gothic detail.

For those of pretended wealth the firm boasted 'All mustards and casters have silver tops, *Hall marked*'. At the same time they suggested that the money saved by not buying silver plate would earn interest in seven years that would pay for similar goods in electroplate.

The main worry to the housewife of course was that with hard use the silver plating soon rubbed away showing the ugly grey nickel basis. Only the Mappin & Webb Prince's plate, marked 'Triple Deposit', was guaranteed to wear like sterling silver for twenty years. For the rest, worn goods could be replated. A tea and coffee set for example, might cost a pound or so, including regilding inside the cream and sugar vessels. Alas, fine Sheffield plate has often been mistreated in this way.

The Elkingtons, who were leading silversmiths as well as making electroplate, employed Continental designers in the

An Elkington electrotype replica in silver of the shield, *The Battle of the Amazons*, from the original by Antoine Vechte. 1871. Text page 107.

exuberant manner of the 1840s. Even in electroplate they could offer a prestige piece such as a thirty-guinea épergne with stags on a rocky base around a tree hung with glass dishes, or with cherubs among vines. 'Moorish' Arabs and date palms too had a remarkably lasting appeal to mid Victorians.

Through the 1870s and 1880s, however, a number of reforming influences affected even commercial design. Shapes became taller and plainer long before end-of-century Art Nouveau, including stemmed tall-handled vessels for tea and coffee engraved with classical figure scenes. Pleasant urn outlines might be exaggerated into more angular shapes, however, and some narrow-necked wide-based vessels were given prominent V-shaped handles.

Late Victorian contrasts

This was a period of many interesting and conflicting moods, far beyond the old contrasts of classical grace and Rococo frivolity. Japanese design became important, including plant shapes, and the reforming zeal of such men as Sir Henry Cole began to have effect. In the previous chapter I referred to the starkly functional designs for metal wares by Christopher Dresser. They may be seen in work by the Elkingtons, by the Sheffield firm of James Dixon & Sons and by Hukin & Heath of Birmingham. This period's handworked craft silver was imitated occasionally, too, by toning down the bright silver with a greyish patina and introducing Art Nouveau motifs.

End-of-century catalogues show an enormous range of electroplated table wares (though it is hard to imagine just who bought all the knife rests shaped as greyhounds, sphinxes and the like). Novelties included the plainly useful four-footed breakfast dish with a domed revolving lid that opened by sliding out of the way under the dish, an idea that soon spread to butter pots, egg steamers and so on. This was a period of endless silver-mounted cut glass–claret jugs and biscuit barrels, salad bowls, celery vases and arrays of toilet bottles–and all this glitter could be matched in electroplate.

Prices emphasise the value of such goods to the middle class family, being less than half or even a third of those of solid silver. In the 1890s electroplating on Britannia metal was cheaper even than on nickel silver. This alloy, a kind of lead-free pewter, is described in the next chapter. It is sometimes recognised as the basis for electroplating by the punched letters *EPBM*.

By the 1890s Sheffield plate was all but forgotten. Strangely, just as buttons were among the first items made by Bolsover in 1742, so too they were among the last, early in this century–the last, that is, until collector-interest in this fascinating subject brought inevitable modern reproductions.

Pewter, Brass and Copper

For centuries brass and pewter gleamed a welcome into mansion, farmhouse and merchant's villa, precious as palace gold and silver plate. All who could afford the comfortable luxury turned to these clean sturdy wares for the furnishings of table and kitchen, for lamp and candlestick and for innumerable personal treasures from pipe stopper and snuffbox to handwarmer and coat button.

Only during the past two hundred years have ordinary folk been offered the pleasant serviceable earthenware and plated silver that I have described in previous chapters. But pewter and brass remain from Roman Britain; by the 14th century their manufacture was controlled by powerful guilds. Throughout the centuries that matter to today's collectors—from, say, the 1660s to the 1900s—Britain was at the centre of Europe's metalworking.

Both pewter and brass are alloys, or mixed metals. Just as silver was toughened with a trace of copper, so was silvery tin, to make the finest quality of pewter. Brass is an alloy of copper and zinc. Both overcame unwelcome competition by showing impressive improvements in quality and manufacturing methods, and these aid the collector, although dating can seldom be precise.

Inevitably reproductions abound. Old pewter was 'discovered' by late Victorians, and many early rarities were copied. Copiers of old brass have often looked no further back than to mid Victorian horse brasses, yet even these fakes may be betrayed by a careless finish that no Victorian would have tolerated.

Early pewter

For early pewterers, the guild rules were strict, controlling the sadware men who made plates, the spoonmakers, the tankard

Pewter flagon, early Georgian. This shows a row of small punch marks intended to suggest silver hallmarks below the crowned X quality mark. Text page 112.

and flagon makers long known as potters, and the triflers responsible for many minor articles such as buckles. The temptation always was to make the alloy easier to work by adding lead: this ley metal eventually became so poisonous that a law in 1907 limited the lead content to ten per cent.

A garnish of early pewter is every collector's dream–a set of a dozen each of large platters, plates and bowls. Tin-and-temper–tin hardened with a little copper and bismuth or later antimony–made this gleaming flatware, requiring no surface ornament save the occasional triangle of initials in a marriage plate (surname initial at the apex, husband's and wife's first-name initials below). Variously reeded rims date from the late 17th century onwards, following silver styles. Huge platters were made, 28 inches across, small pie dishes long known as coffins and plain flat trenchers that were placed alongside more valuable dinner plates to take the scratches of meat-cutting.

Compulsory makers' marks made it possible for the guild to identify early pewter, and records of a few of these 'touches' remain. London especially retained quality control well into the 18th century, so that there was pride in the mark 'London made'. But it must be admitted that tiny punchmarks beside the maker's mark were deceitfully intended to suggest silver hallmarks. Factory and pattern-registration numbers, too, were in use by the 19th century, now sometimes mistaken as dates.

Latten and cast brass

Medieval brassmen, too, were called potters when they cast their metal into cooking and serving vessels. Other early brassmen–latteners–noisily hammered their brass ingots into sheets for flatware; latten in church memorial plates offers fascinating glimpses of life and costume from the 13th century. England had water-driven battery hammers flattening brass in the 1580s, but much fine latten was imported until early in the 18th century.

The collector can develop an eye for the colour and texture of early pewter and brass by examining museum specimens. The

Brass wall-sconce, cast and meticulously finished to ensure a gleaming reflection to enhance the candle's light. This is signed *Edward Gore 1706*. Text page 114. Victoria and Albert Museum, London.

hanging chandelier, for example, made for church and livery hall was an assembly of brass castings–sockets, grease pans, finely scrolling arms and a shapely central body topped by an ornamental finial and based in a hollow reflective globe. Countless early brass kitchen vessels and tools included long-handled skimmers and the three-footed saucepans (posnets) required for the open down-hearth. The curfew, shaped as a quarter sphere, recalls the medieval edict that such fires should be covered at night and saved wearisome relighting in the morning. Early brass lanterns might have cheap bull's-eye panels from the glass factory.

Pewter and brass contributed especially richly to the 17th- and early 18th-century home. Wall shelves would be bright with reflective well-scoured pewter, while embossed brass magnified the light of candles in scrolling wall sconces. Everywhere there would be pewter and brass candlesticks, with snuffers to trim the wicks and douters to extinguish them.

Manufacturing methods

The ways these pieces were made are important to the collector who quickly sees that casting was at the heart of most early work. Molten metal was poured into moulds so costly that they often had to be hired from the guilds. Even pewter plates were cast before being trimmed in the lathe and hand hammered to make the metal compact and rigid, especially around the curve of the bouge. A final smoothing and burnishing then obliterated marks from the upper surface.

Where necessary a piece could be soldered (paling to the pewterer and brazing to the brassman). For example, a 17th-century candlestick would be cast in parts and finished by lathe-turning. In pewter the candlestick base mould might serve also for casting salt cellars. Like silver too the earliest brass and pewter spoons had gay little cast finials–lion, acorn, maidenhead–soldered to straight stems and well-hammered fig-shaped bowls. In the later 17th century these were followed by notched flattened ends including treasured rarities cast with embossed surface ornament.

Pewter and brass continued to share with iron all the duties of increasingly sophisticated domesticity into early Georgian days. Design pleases us with its simplicity, but there is much ingenious ornament to watch for. Records of early pewterers' fines tell us that at least some broke the rules by attempting to gild their wares. Occasionally, too, brass was given colourful ornament, being cast with tiny surface hollows to be filled with enamel colours.

Prince's metal

The more familiar gilding that gave a permanent brilliance to the finest ornamental brass, such as furniture mounts, was a more obvious early way for men to improve its tone. More interestingly, in the 17th century a type with a greater proportion of copper to zinc was known as Prince Rupert's metal or prince's metal. This was not very different from the invention of Christopher Pinchbeck, a watchmaker, who probably used tutenag, the refined Chinese zinc that came to this country lining cases of tea. Pinchbeck, the metal, was widely advertised by Christopher's son in the 1730s and 1740s. It was slow to tarnish and popular for inexpensive jewellery and bijouterie. But soon the name was applied indiscriminately to cheaply gilded brass.

Traditional ornament

Most generally effective on both brass and pewter was raised ornament, sometimes complemented by engraving although collectors must beware of later 'improvements'. Here the influence came from the silversmiths who gave an extra sparkle to candlestick or tankard with such light-catching embellishments as the repetitive border swellings known as gadroons. Occasionally quite elaborate ornament cast in relief is found on spoon or handled bowl.

Joggled or wriggled work ornamenting a pewter punch bowl. Diameter 8 inches. Early 18th century. Text page 116.

This page: Brass caster of about 1700, with ornamental piercing comparable with the period's silver patterns. Text below. Victoria and Albert Museum, London.

Opposite page: Late 18th-century brass strike-light, for table use. When 'fired' like a flint-lock pistol it ignited tinder in the pan which could then be used to light a 'match' stored in the weapon's barrel. Text opposite page. The Royal Pavilion, Art Gallery and Museum, Brighton.

The engraver's ornament of delicate lines cut into the metal surface was largely confined to showy brasswork, for example on clock faces. In pewter such engraving soon became indistinct and so may have been more common than we know: as early as Elizabethan days the Pewterers' Guild twice fined a man for employing a woman (not a Guild member) to engrave his ware. The work that has lasted is mainly the crude wriggled or joggled ornament with outlines chipped out in tiny zigzags. Derisive silver engravers called this 'scratching'. Even simpler repetitive patterns were made sometimes on both pewter and brass with hammer and tiny punches.

More interesting ornament was created by perforating the metal. In pewter this is to be found in the cast handles of the small bowls now usually called porringers and long known as counterfeits from their resemblance to silver, and in the vertical thumbpiece or lever that gives character to the lidded tankard. In brass some of the most splendid work was cast and engraved on locks and keys. These included chamberlains' keys-of-office, for example, and superb lockplates where surface engraving might be combined with delicate cast tracery.

Closely following gilded silver, thin brass sheet was pierced in the dainty arabesque patterns of the early 18th century.

Vessels include casters and the spherical soap or wash-ball holders used on early washbasin stands.

Birmingham brass

For brass the 18th-century success story is associated mainly with Birmingham where brass was first made no earlier than 1740; forty years later the town used a thousand tons a year. A much improved form of brass became available to mid Georgians who welcomed this lovely golden Emerson 'spelter brass'. This was a splendid time for brassware, changing like silver from the mid century's lively Rococo scrolls to the suave grace of the Neo-classical vogue led by Robert Adam from the 1760s.

Candlesticks and candelabra are found, and the saucer-shaped chamber candlestick fitted with a pair of snuffers, perhaps, and a cone extinguisher. Springs to make snuffers trim the candles more cleanly came in 1749, followed by various patented notions until snuffers gradually went out of use in early Victorian days with the improvement in candlewick weaving. The smoker's wax-jack was popular, in brass as well as silver (page 97) burning with a safe tiny flame. The pistol-shaped strike-light is a welcome find, too, as are brass and pewter pipe stoppers, snuffboxes and snuff-rasps.

Matthew Boulton, 1728–1809, of Birmingham was a leading figure in late 18th-century factory achievement. He was renowned for a refined gilded brass used for ornaments, cande-

labra and lavish furniture mounts. By then casting methods had improved, but there were other ways too for handling this fine brass. Improved rolling mills could flatten it into thin level sheets, and improved steel in new stamping machines could shape and pattern it.

Georgian copper and pewter

Finely rolled copper must come into the story here. The metal was always an important ingredient of brassy alloys, but its welcoming warm glow only gradually became a feature of mid Georgian hearthside and kitchen. A Georgian copper warming pan for example was lighter than the early brass pan but far sturdier than the usual reproduction. Most familiar is the design with a 'beefeater hat' lid: in late machine-stamped copper the lid rim fits inside the ember pan rim. The hot-water bottle type, filled by unscrewing at the handle socket, was evolved around 1770, and here as so often the collector may find the useful notion expressed in pewter too.

Some table and kitchen wares were made in copper too, of

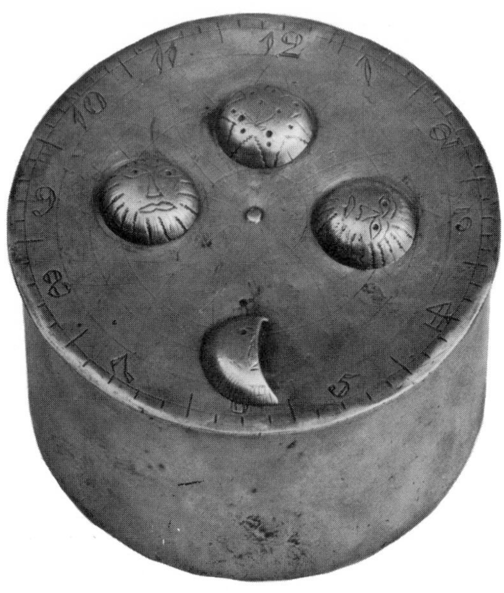

Heavy copper table snuffbox. One of many ingenious designs developed by watchmakers of Prescot when the French undercut their trade in watch units. A would-be pilferer would have to manipulate the domed sun, moon and stars to unlock the lift-off lid. The locking mechanism was protected from the snuff by a metal plate and the whole interior heavily tinned. Such boxes are collected as Lancashire snuffboxes, typically with watch-dial numerals around the rim.

course, all needing frequent interior tinning, but far more date to the 19th century after copper was freed from war-needs restrictions.

Through the 18th century the emphasis still was on fine pewter wares such as become available to the collector from time to time. The range is wide, including more plates, saucers (still for serving sauce) and the little dishes hired out for informal parties called dessert or banqueting dishes. Pewter, pleasantly smooth and clean to the lips, was especially valued for drinking vessels, the old guild rules stipulating that all interiors must be lathe burnished.

Vessels include the church flagon, important from the 1600s, tall, broad-skirted and tapering, with decorative thumbpiece and lid finial and, in the 18th century, sometimes an elaborate double-scroll handle. Following the 17th century's straight-sided, wide-skirted style, Georgian tankards included the attractive waisted tulip shape associated with West Country pewter. This has a domed cover and an attractive curl or double curl to the tail of the handle that continued into early Victorian days. The open thumbpiece with a cut-away centre was an 18th-century favourite before the tankard lost its final style of rimless lid.

A vessel restricted wholly to pewter was the flat-lidded baluster wine measure, which can be dated roughly by the style of its thumbpiece and lid attachment. Careful scrutiny can suggest at least half a dozen ways that its design helped the customer to detect any reduction in size such as dents made by a cunning barman.

The 'potbellied' or pear-shaped measure was a Scottish variant, with a lid like an inverted saucer, rarer today than the tappit hen. This popular name has been given to measures of all capacities but strictly meant a Scottish pint (three Imperial pints), smaller sizes being the chopin and mutchkin. The tappit hen has a much deeper vertical rim than the English measure, and instead of the smooth baluster swell the body is concave down to a low waist and below this is vertical-sided again.

Many other attractive Georgian pewter items remain such as the writing box then known as a standish. Beakers and loving cups may be noted in simple versions of silver design. But improving earthenwares for the table had a disastrous effect on mid Georgian pewterers so that many attempted to cut prices by using heavily leaded 'thundercloud' alloys.

Depression was soon followed, however, by a new era of widespread success. It is fascinating to trace how both pewter and brass triumphed in the great 'modern' industrial expansion that became important late in the 18th century.

Britannia metal

In pewter the pioneer was John Vickers of Britannia Place, Sheffield, who from 1769 began making a ware much like the early lead-free pewter (mainly tin with a little bluish antimony and copper), calling it Vickers white metal. Cream jugs, tobacco boxes, beakers and teapots have been found impressed with his name. His stronger variant became important from the early 1790s. This is known as hard pewter or Britainnia metal, and by 1817 Sheffield alone had over seventy makers, the Dixon firm being among the most important. Britannia metal, originally burnished bright as silver, is so like fine early pewter that the collector distinguishes it mainly by the way it was handled by the machine age.

Hearthside brassware

The early years of the 19th century saw power-driven machines rolling and stamping all these metals. In brass this meant that machine-embossed surface patterns could be included on many drawer handles, for instance, and repetitive perforations in small furniture galleries, although often cast ornament was still preferred such as cast handles and feet. Perforated patterns are found in many an attractive trivet among especially collectable hearthside bygones.

Trivets and toasters and other brasses served the coal-burning grate in the Georgian and Victorian living room. The trivet to stand in the hearth, with three legs or four, was affectionately known as the footman or jonathan; others, one-legged, hooked inside the fender or on the bars of the grate. Here was a spot for the brass or copper tea kettle or for the Britannia metal muffin dish, perhaps, which would be accompanied on the tea-table by a small cinnamon dredger or muffineer.

Urns in all these metals followed fashionable silver shapes. A patent of 1774 had introduced the long-favoured box-iron for keeping the contents hot through a leisurely breakfast: a small iron bar was heated in the kitchen fire and put in a central vertical 'box' inside the urn.

Regency brilliance

So much was happening to these metals around the turn of the century and into Regency and late Georgian years that it is a wonderful period for the collector. In brass unusual specialist collections include the scores of different brass emblems carried in their magnificent annual processions by village friendly societies. These 'rainy day' savings societies proliferated after an act of 1793. The emblems are usually found cast in flat silhouette, such as shepherds' crooks. Buttons challenge the collector to recognise and date not only their ornament but the different ways their shanks were fixed.

Around the house, door-stops had become necessary after a self-closing door mechanism was introduced in 1775. At first the brass 'door porter' was just a solid little ornament on a long handle but from the 1790s a flat-back shape was placed close against the door, whether unimaginative half handbell or lively Neo-classical lion, sphinx or winged chimera. These were followed in the 1820s–1830s by horses, hounds and the early Victorians' celebrity figures and favourite bird-and-snake.

More surprising to some collectors is the late arrival of the cast brass door knocker. These lion heads with ring rappers, Medusa heads with foliage festoons and sphinx heads with lyres seldom date earlier than Regency days (and inevitably now are widely reproduced).

Door porter, the horse screwed to a heavy plinth; a design that could be moved with one's toe without stooping. These are found in iron as well as brass, often with a bronzed finish. Text page 121.

Copper is associated with magnificent late Georgian and Victorian kitchen wares, ladles, skimmers, cheese toasters, egg poachers. The oval vessels for cooking fish were known as kettles, but the copper kettle with spout and bail handle is such an endearing article that it has never gone out of production. The Regency's superb Neo-classical copper urn was followed by flamboyant early Victorian shapes in tall vase outline with fussy legs and handle details.

Britannia metal too was immensely popular through the 19th century. Collectors look for all kinds of useful wares from glass-lined mustard pots to those plates with Britannia metal linings containing hot water to keep the dinner warm. They are reminded of the metal's original bright shine by the period's pleasure in such status symbols as visiting card trays, fruit baskets and cruet frames. Teapots and the like might be cast in complicated many-part moulds, but more often the collector finds a vessel in thin metal made in parts by stamping for assembly with solder. Melon shaping and turned-over edges strengthened it, and for impressive weight it might be almost overwhelmed by its added load of cast ornamental vines or shells or oakleaves.

One of the most important advances, however, meant that lightweight inexpensive vessels in all these metals could be shaped by the process known as spinning as described in the previous chapter.

Lamps and candles

All the paraphernalia of early 19th-century lighting has a great appeal for collectors. Candlesticks in all the metals changed from severe Neo-classical outlines to renewed flamboyance. They included the thick-stemmed straight telescopic candlesticks patented in 1796 and the bedroom sticks with tall glass shades requiring the long-handled extinguishers that sometimes turn up. Lamps ranged from the classic Roman floating wick style to the Swiss-patented Argand lamp introduced in the early 1780s. The period's sluggish vegetable and fish oils prompted designs with handsome urn-shaped fonts above the projecting burners. The moderator lamp with a regulated oil flow came in 1836. Meanwhile dangerous benzine had been discovered in 1825, but the blessing of paraffin came only in 1861.

Victorian exuberance

Revived Rococo scrolling, lavish naturalistic flower and vine ornament and contrasts of matt and burnished surfaces enabled brass and Britannia metal to hold their own in the bright, cluttered Victorian home. As in china and silver, the typical Britannia metal teapot and matching vessels for coffee, milk and sugar were in long-necked, heavy-bodied outlines. Spout and feet tended to sag or sprawl but were rich in lively detail.

Even the fireside fender and poker, tongs and shovel–the brasses that were 'done' each dawn by an under-housemaid–shared the current enthusiasm for naturalistic flora and fauna. In 1838, however, the Gothic architect, A. W. N. Pugin (1812–1852) became Birmingham's first designer of art brass, and his

Medieval Court at the 1851 Great Exhibition prompted lasting interest in antique brass design.

At a more popular level both brass and pewter appeared among the period's pairs of figures sold as cheap chimney ornaments which included miniature replicas of household furnishings. Many more of these appealing tinies were carefully made by specialists in enormous quantities for dolls and dolls' houses —coal scuttles, coffee pots and the rest. One proud maker of such miniatures in 1852 described his copper kettle as being composed of sixteen pieces yet sold for sixpence, so perfect that it was 'fit to boil water in, or cook anything you like'.

Horse brass caution

Horse brasses are so widely collected as fireside ornaments that they demand a mention despite the fact that very few date earlier than mid Victorian days. Indeed many sold today (single-piece castings in common industrial brass) betray their newness by a careless finish and artificially induced signs of wear bearing no relation to the way they would be rubbed as they swung on the dray or wagon harness. Ever since Roman days men have sought protection for their horses by dazzling the evil eye. The forehead facepiece, for example, was a domed latten disc by the 18th century and a cast hand-finished sun with serrated edge from the 1820s. It might appear with drilled perforations until the 1870s when it was shaped by a single die-stamping in thin rolled brass, finished at first with careful hand filing.

Similar changes in production methods can be traced in a collection of the most familiar martingale brasses—at York Castle Museum, for instance. The collector notes too a late Victorian change in subject to many lacking any association with a driven horse or its owner and to souvenir portraits.

Art wares

Basically the collector has, as ever, to recognise the colour and feel of his brass, and this applies to every aspect of metalwork. Late Victorian and Edwardian catalogues offered an endless

Horse shoes, wheatsheaves, acorns, thistles and two rows of commemorative designs on horse brasses from the extensive collection in the Castle Museum, York. Text opposite page.

variety of brass and copper wares such as ornamental tea-kettles and gongs, paraffin lamps and bedrooms jugs, easily mistaken today for mid century work. Other items such as realistic lobster and tortoise inkstands defiantly declare their period. Most dangerous perhaps are self-conscious 'art wares', some offered early this century with a 'tarnished' finish to suggest antiques, together with long out-of-fashion brass pipe stoppers and mantelshelf figures of Dickens characters.

In contrast, such important designers as W. A. S. Benson and Christopher Dresser, whom I have mentioned earlier, welcomed the cheap thinly rolled metals for designs of forward-looking functional severity. Collectors today particularly enjoy some of the late Victorian and Edwardian efforts by Arts and Crafts enthusiasts then busy with metalwork in countless groups up and down the country. The brass and copper they have left us ranges from obvious trays and rosebowls to repoussé furniture plaques and door finger-plates, firescreens, newly fashionable menu holders and photograph frames set with richly coloured pottery 'Ruskin stones'.

Amateurs were encouraged to take up the craft by those who obligingly supplied the materials and finished off their efforts. But at the end of the collectors' period as at the beginning some of the most interesting work was supplied by the new generation of pewterers.

Britannia metal continued in vast demand for briefly shining table wares from toast-racks to tea and coffee sets, including Georgian designs. But it was the soft traditional pewter that was especially welcomed by late Victorian aesthetes. By then this was a very minor ware for such items as tankards and ice pudding moulds. Interest was renewed when the Lord Mayor of London in 1885 was head of London's one remaining pewter manufactory, Brown & Englefield. As a past Master Pewterer he included a craft display in the Lord Mayor's Show, with suitably costumed pewterers tossing souvenir medals to the crowds.

Books on old pewter soon followed, and the collector has to remember that many traditional patterns were revived to confuse us today. But the metal lent itself especially to the rhythmical, unacademic patterns of Art Nouveau. The veriest amateur quickly discovered how easy it was to tool the soft metal into buttons, hatpin heads and the like. The Liberty firm issued Tudric pewter from 1902 including simplified versions of its Cymric silver (chapter 6), and other manufacturers shared in the new fashion for 'art pewter' clock cases, trinket sets, photo frames, mirror backs and the like to compete with imports of be-dragoned Japanese 'antimony ware'.

All this renewed activity brings problems to the collector seeking genuine early wares. But it may be consoling to recall how Victorians themselves were happily duped by extraordinarily naive figurines and medallions cast in the cheapest pewter and lead in imagined ancient designs. These were made and 'discovered' in the Thames mud by William Smith and Charles Eaton. They were shown up as fakes in 1858 but are now affectionately collected as Billies and Charlies.

Pewter in combination with ebony used to ornament an oak dining chair in the manner widely approved around 1900. Text opposite page.

Miscellanea

So far I have touched upon only the major subjects that interest beginner-collectors of antiques in wood, ceramics and metals. But there is so much more for the finding, in so many other attractive materials. Here I can only suggest a few that have endured down the centuries as welcome reminders of further craftsman skills and fashion foibles. Among these the collector tends to turn to the small elegancies that men and women wore or carried, especially during the 18th and 19th centuries. Here my concern is not so much with wealth-declaring jewelled gold as with the minor items wherein specialist craftsmen reflected rich fashion by their brilliant handling of less exclusive materials.

English painted enamels

These appeared as substantial candlesticks and cased sets of tea caddies, as mustard pots and perforated counter trays, but they are associated especially with elegant little adult 'toys'. In the 18th century these toys included thimble cases and the like to hang from the chatelaine, snuffboxes, steel-mirrored patch boxes, etuis, smelling-bottles, miniature writing sets, pocket nutmeg graters and sweet boxes or bonbonnières. In painted enamels (as in Sheffield plate, for instance) the collector finds cut-price imitations of society's fashionable glitter.

The example was set by the wealthy Georgians' portrait

miniatures painted enduringly in enamel colours on snuffboxes of jewelled gold. But the term English painted enamels today implies commercial work produced under go-ahead factory conditions. The painting was still by hand, of course, but often slight and sometimes over transfer outlines, and the clear white enamel ground (toughened opacified glass) was fused on to a strong core of extremely thin copper. Yet the colours are as fresh today as when they were new, and so fine was typical craftsmanship that even for snuff powder no box ever required a fastening to secure the hinged lid.

The craft's early history is obscure, but it appears to have been well established before Battersea in London acquired a reputation for plaques, snuffboxes, decanter labels and the like.

Painted enamel etui partitioned to contain manicure tools, pencil, memoranda slip of ivory, etc. The case is oval on plan, the deep lid hinged narrowly on the left and opened by a press stud on the right, with tooled gilt-metal rims to the opening and around the top and base. South Staffordshire, about 1760s–70s. Text opposite page.

The venture there lasted only from 1753 to 1756, and collectors now realise that the main sources of these small charmers were Birmingham and the Bilston-Wednesbury area of South Staffordshire. Battersea's fame depended on delicate one-colour printed ornament. This was achieved by expert and then highly novel use of transfer papers to convey a special kind of printer's ink from copper plate engravings to the smooth white enamel surface, the technique that has dominated ornament on ceramic table wares ever since. The Midlands craftsmen tended to prefer more colourful flower posies and classical landscape scenes—all the themes currently in vogue including portraits copied from popular prints—with hand-painted colours often obscuring transfer-printed outlines. Published patterns for decorators were available, but it is surprisingly rare today among genuine specimens to identify a source, let alone to find any duplicates.

To understand these decorators' skill it must be realised that each of several colours would require a separate, expertly controlled oven firing to reveal its tone and give it permanence and brilliance. The Midlands enamellers often also coloured the whole surface of the enamel, pink or turquoise, deep blue or yellow and then diapered it to please the user's fingers with lines of raised enamel dots. White reserves left for the main painted ornament then needed to be framed, so gay scrolling was introduced, being a late reminder of the Rococo vogue still popular with commercial engravers. These asymmetrical flourishes were painted in raised white enamel and brilliantly gilded by the dangerous mercury process developed in the 1760s.

Because the enamel paste adhered most easily when its copper core was slightly curved the early wares consisted mainly of slightly convex plaques and the boxes that could be composed of similarly convex shapes framed up in strips of finely tooled and gilded metal. But a wider range of items could be made when the copper core was shaped by heavy presses and merely dipped in spilly opaque-enamel. Popular items such as the boxes for comfits shaped and enamelled as crouching parrots and finches show how successful this became. Even candlesticks could be made, in screwed-together parts, and snuffboxes appeared in attractive waisted shapes with metal strip confined to the rims. Sadly, however, towards the century's end came rapid deterioration, due in part to loss of the export trade to war-torn Europe. Many a give-away box that remains showing a minimum of metalwork and hasty painted ornament is a poor little representative of past glories.

Tortoiseshell and ivory

These were most skilfully fashioned into a comparable range of small personal treasures down the centuries before wild life conservationists became aware of the havoc that might be involved. Like painted enamel the tortoiseshell's smooth, flavour-free, untarnishable surfaces were ideal for boxing snuff and breath-sweetening comfits or cashews, and for vessels such as cups and scent flasks. The lightness and warmth to the fingers made the shell uniquely welcome for small jewellery, fan sticks and the shuttles used in the netting and tatting that shortened many a tedious journey. Here however is a material that needs the constant gentle handling more natural in yesterday's world than today's.

Tortoiseshell box showing effective application of gold in the range of ornament known as piqué. Early 19th century. Text page 132.

The finest transparent shell came from the hawksbill turtle, pale or blond tortoiseshell being favoured late in the 18th century. The great Birmingham manufacturer Matthew Boulton widened the craft's possibilities by invisibly heat-welding thin pieces of the shell to produce sheet tortoiseshell for large table snuffboxes and the like. He introduced the delicate surface incisions known as engine turning and heated the shell to shape patterns in deep relief. But most collectors look especially for tortoiseshell shimmering with patterns in dots of shining gold.

This ornament came to England in the late 17th century with Huguenot refugees and has retained its French name of piqué d'or. Patterns in larger dots were known as nailhead or clouté d'or. The boldest style composed of strip gold inlay was posé d'or although this too may now sell as piqué.

Early Georgians following French fashions had an especial love of this posé d'or with its chinoiseries and pastoral scenes and romantic figure groups, sometimes with the gold detail exquisitely tooled. No cement was required: patterns cut from the paper-thin pure gold – or silver – were laid upon the heated shell which, as it cooled, contracted and gripped the metal so firmly that the whole surface could be polished and burnished to a silky gloss.

The craft continued successfully in Birmingham and Sheffield far into the 19th century, becoming notably flamboyant in the 1820s with different tones of gold. So considerable became the popularity of Victorian piqué jewellery (crosses, brooches, earrings) that it was even imitated in gilt metal and celluloid.

The tiny rods of gold or silver were inserted into ivory too. This ornament also is known as piqué, often set off by staining the ivory green, blue, black or red. It is still found today in the knobs and hooks of Edwardian parasol handles (matched of course by the spoke tips).

Ivory, however, has far more to offer the collector. Its superbly silken surface may be recognised by minute lines in lozenge shapes, differentiating it from splintery bone. Experts further distinguish close-textured, glossy African ivory from the more densely white, easily worked Indian, and both from the hard white 'seahorse ivory' of hippopotamus teeth and from all those sea creatures' teeth naively engraved by sailors or their modern copyists and sold now as scrimshaw work. Even so-called vegetable ivory from the stones of a species of palm was popular early this century, being turned into buttons, draughts and thimbles.

The unique flexible toughness of elephant ivory has been proved spectacularly in carved and pierced work – in paper-thin brisé fans, for example, composed wholly of ivory threaded with ribbons. Some would claim that such manual dexterity drew attention away from the skill of the creative artist carving delicate portrait medallions. This skill was somewhat undermined also by such mid Victorian marvels as the Cheverton carving machine that provided the uncritical with fashionable ivory busts and bas reliefs.

Clever lathe-turned ornament was popular from the 18th century including the turned and drilled balls-within-balls made in Europe as well as in China. But purists may prefer the pleasure of handling simple ivory counters such as the abun-

Brisé fan composed wholly of ivory linked around the edge with ribbons. Painted medallions and intricate carving suggest silk and lace but in fact each blade is a single unit from rivet to border. Late 18th century. Text above. Victoria and Albert Museum, London.

dant flat fish shapes, and the ivory veneers on innumerable tea caddies, snuffboxes and workboxes (fitted of course with exquisite fretted silk winders, needlecases and the rest). Here especially there is scope for today's collector. By the 1850s ivory veneer could be cut in continuous strip round and round the tusk.

Perhaps the most enduring favourites, however, are found among Victorian playthings–the ivory warriors on the chess-board, the tiny saws, mallets and the like to be extricated from a haphazard pile in the game of spillikins and the minute furnishings–'a hundred to fit in a cherry stone'–offered by the traditional ivory carvers of Dieppe.

Mother of pearl

All shimmering iridescent shells shared with tortoiseshell and ivory in pleasing the lily-white fingers of our more affluent late Georgian and Victorian ancestors. But the story is far older. Ancient Egyptians enjoyed pearly inlays, and gold-mounted nautilus shell cups were the pride of early European civilisation. Table vessels and furnishings remain from Tudor and Stuart days covered with small scales of pearly shell, forerunners of all the gorgeous fan sticks, snuffboxes and other delights, fretted and carved and foil-enriched, that contributed to 18th-century splendour.

Most familiar today perhaps are the early Victorians' pearl-handled posy holder and the long-popular visiting card case, too slender even to hold today's cigarettes. In this, a velvet-lined boxwood frame may be surface-patterned with shell in diamond shapes, often in contrasting pinky-white and blue-green tones or with panels of low relief carving or lines of tortoiseshell. The shell was obtained as the innermost lining of various seashells including the pearl oyster, its natural structure producing the iridescence. The most radiant was the snail-shaped nautilus, while the most consistently silvery white was found in huge Australian shells introduced around the mid 19th century, sometimes spoilt by a hint of yellow.

Collectors note increasingly expert handling of the shell as Victorians imitated even the nautilus cups and the Tudor scale ornament riveted to metal and glued to wood. This was thicker and less lustrous than the early work, however, and shaped by grinding rather than the old hand filing. So great was the material's appeal that even the waste was powdered, filtered and bottled with lemon juice to sell as a beauty wash for the complexion.

Shell cameos

Shell cameos were introduced as a particularly interesting and now highly valued development of the vast trade in colourful shells. These were carved in slightly convex portions of conch shells. Fashionable Europe's interest in substantial classical ornament around the beginning of the 19th century gave

Shell cameo brooch finely carved against a tawny orange background, the maenad or follower of Bacchus showing all the legendary features–head thrown back, rounded face with dreamy expression, fruiting vine in dishevelled hair, and carrying a thyrsus staff headed with a pine cone. Text above. Mrs W. Hopley.

impetus to the craft in Italy. As early as 1805 fashion comment recommended carved shells as a substitute for antique cameo stones, and by the 1840s in England the craft had reached its heyday: by the 1860s quality was deteriorating with only a minor revival for small jewellery in the late 1880s.

Typically the shell's golden yellow or orange-red lining formed the background to ornament carved in a whitish central layer revealed when the outermost casing was cut away. But colour varied widely in shells from different oceans. With cutting tools, files and scrapers the carver removed unwanted white shell from the richly coloured background and carved his tiny figure scene or profile head in extremely low relief.

Even the itinerant cameo carver seeking individual commissions rarely attempted true portrait likenesses in the silhouette manner. The collector most usually finds heads of gods and goddesses or familiar themes from classical mythology, with nothing to indicate their country of origin and only the mount to suggest a date. Much of the skill lay in taking advantage of the curved shape of a piece of shell and chance irregularities in colour and surface. Final smoothing with pumice and polishing with rottenstone left the cameo ready for mounting in brooch or bracelet, sometimes with matching necklace and earrings.

Marble

Marble is another decorative substance associated with Italy and suited to early 19th-century archaeological interests. This proved remarkably successful for a time in Derbyshire around such small townships as Matlock, Bakewell and Ashford-in-the-Water. Derbyshire's sparkling gemstone fluorspar has always been unique to Castleton, its appealing amethyst-and-honey colours earning it the name blue-john from French importers. When William Duesbury, the Derby potter, introduced it to London in about 1770 it proved vastly successful in handsome urn and tazza ornaments; but the main deep seams were soon exhausted, and the region found more lasting success with their more widely distributed marbles. These included the glowing

Derbyshire marble inlay. Ornaments turned in glossy black Ashford marble and delicately inlaid with flower patterns. 19th century. Text below.

unflecked 'black jack', so soft and easily worked that it was even exported to Italy, and others ranging in colour from 'rosewood' to soft pinks, yellows, browns, greens and greys, many patterned with shell and fossil.

These marbles were made into the usual run of souvenirs for the late Georgians and early Victorians who toured the lovely Derbyshire dales, but the collector finds special interest in the clever local crafts prompted by the material. At first scraps of marble were fitted together to make haphazard veneers, but soon neatly fitting geometrical patterns made the most of the contrasting colours, textures and fossil detail in veneers cemented over a marble base.

More importantly, from the 1830s, complicated inlays proved successful. Tiny pieces cut from local marbles and spars were set into hollows cut in the black marble to represent the early Victorians' adored flower posies, butterflies and birds. Collectors search for tables in this Derbyshire inlay and panels for furniture and clocks as well as smaller items such as tea caddies, chessboards and desk fittings. The Duke of Devonshire lent the men specimens of Italian *pietra dura* from nearby Chatsworth, but the Derbyshire inlays retained their local character until their makers were tempted to emphasise the complexity of their work by introducing a wider range of colours with pieces of malachite, lapis lazuli, glass and so on.

The trouble by then was that the simpler marble mosaics were in production in several parts of Britain and Derbyshire had competitors as far apart as Cornwall's Lizard and Connemara. Nevertheless the real enemy proved to be the high cost of complicated inlays. A price-cutting substitute was already in view at the 1851 Great Exhibition where the Derbyshire men won several prizes. This was painted slate, its flower ornament hardened by long oven heating. High claims were made for its strength, comparative lightness and durability by Magnus of Pimlico and other makers, but it is seldom encountered today.

Paper

At the other extreme, would-be collectors find some of their most fragile yet liveliest collectable treasure in paper. Valentines gave substance to what was already ancient custom when they were first offered for sale in the 1760s. The flimsy early folded paper sheet became a fascinating complexity of professional ornament when amorous Victorians sent each other elaborations of paper lace, scented artificial flowers, tinselled pictures, transformation scenes and even relief effects so three-dimensional that they had to be mounted on tiny paper springs in special boxes. These are collectors' treasure indeed. But in contrast there was some crude and occasionally cruel humour about, too, when the penny post of 1840 made it easier for the sender to remain anonymous.

Surprisingly, Christmas cards began to be offered for sale only in the 1840s and date mainly from the 1860s onwards. The glitter of glass frosting was introduced in 1867, and cards with religious themes came mainly from the late 1870s, followed by the more elaborate three-dimensional picture scenes and four-page booklets in the 1880s. Like paper scraps, the Christmas

Typical of George Baxter in sentimental vein. Printed from 12 colour blocks and edged with gilt for framing. The wording at the bottom reminds the viewer that he had patented this method of oil colour printing. This print was one of five illustrations in Suttaby's *Le Souvenir* published in 1847 at 1s. 6d. and may be found also on sheet music. $3\frac{1}{8} \times 4\frac{3}{4}$ inches. Text below. Mrs E. Ansell.

card trade was dominated by the vivid German full-colour printing known as the chromolithograph, although some delightfully restrained English designs came from such popular illustrators as Kate Greenaway.

Collectors interested in English printing are more likely to enthuse over the phenomenal success of Baxter prints (patented 1836). This is justified, for George Baxter, 1804–67, was a perfectionist as well as a pioneer. His boast was that he used oil colours to print subtle natural tints (no hand touching-up). But much of his skill lay in designing and engraving in aquatint, etching and stipple the plates that printed the basic picture in perfectly shaded monochrome. Over this, colour was printed from a series of equally well prepared and exactly placed wood or soft-metal blocks.

Subjects range from large historical scenes and sentimental stories to minor works for sheet music and the like. The would-be collector has to learn the different ways Baxter signed and sealed his mounted prints (here the British Museum collection is helpful). Also to recognise the work of the engravers licensed to use his process from 1849, especially Abraham Le Blond. Prints sold as Le Blond Baxters were less meticulously printed by Le Blond from Baxter's plates and blocks after 1867, but the vogue for Baxter prints early this century has left us with many an inferior fake.

Picture ribbons

Among the most endearing of the smaller prints were the sets for pasting on needleboxes, now known, confusingly perhaps, as needleprints. This is a term sometimes given also to the extraordinarily detailed print-like pictures in coloured silks known to collectors of Victoriana as Coventry loom-woven picture ribbons. Some of these at the time were called Stevengraphs.

Coventry had a long history of ribbon weaving before the early 19th-century Jacquard loom improvement enabled the weavers to produce multicoloured patterns automatically. 'Landscapes, figures, portraits' were on show at the 1851 Great Exhibition, but it was at the 1862 exhibition that Thomas Stevens had a machine on view making popular ribbon souvenirs. Today collectors enjoy many of the small items he and his rivals issued through the later 19th century. By 1875 he listed as many as five hundred subjects for his 'illuminated pure silk woven book markers', and there were Christmas cards, too, and valentines and scent sachets.

Most familiar are the little pictures such as racing scenes measuring six by two inches, their bevelled gilt-edged cardboard mounts appropriately titled. Brighter than any watercolours, the glossy silks gleam with every change of light, the extremely fine weaving of the background detail subduing the colour to convey a sense of distance behind the vivid foreground activity where the bright colour is emphasised in the heavy broché weaving stitch. Experience soon warns the collector away from a later series with loose stitches in less attractive colouring.

Embroidery

The picture ribbon is of course manifestly factory skill. An entirely different world is open to the collector who seeks old embroideries expressing the needlewoman's pleasure in giving beauty and often a more enduring surface to fabrics such as cushions, counterpanes, wall hangings and many items of dress. In substantial tent stitch she vied with costly woven tapestry; in most persuasive delicate white work, exactly differentiated as drawn, pulled and cut thread work, she rivalled the subtleties of lace. This is far too wide and fascinating a subject to be dismissed in a paragraph. Here I can do no more than urge would-be collectors to look beyond such obvious items as laborious children's samplers and Berlin wool cross stitch–to dress aprons, say, or men's waistcoats, or baby caps or patchwork, until perhaps the handling of such needle beauty may prompt a joyous struggle to do it too.

Fine professional work on a man's waistcoat of the later 18th century in about 20 shades on cream corded silk. The pattern scoffs at men's obsession with waistcoat buttons by working the theme into the border edging and semé ground–and then embroidering the actual buttons to match. Text above. Mary Ireland Collection.

Index

Page numbers in bold type refer to illustrations

Acknowledgments

The Publishers wish to thank the following for the use of photographs: Mrs E. Ansell p. 139. Bracher and Sydenham, Reading p. 85. Brighton Borough Council p. 117. Castle Museum, York p. 125. Cecil Davis Ltd., London p. 64. Christie, Manson and Woods, London pp. 29, 55, 63. Delomosne and Son, London pp. 36, 50, 66, 69. Dudley Metropolitan Borough p. 74. Harris Museum and Art Gallery, Preston pp. 72, 73. Heal and Son, London p. 27. Mrs W. Hopley p. 135. Mrs M. Ireland pp. 58, 141. Mallett and Son, London pp. 14, 19. Norman Adams Ltd., London p. 15. Messrs Preston Ltd., Bolton p. 101. Richard Ogden Ltd., London p. 88. Sheffield City Museum pp. 95, 99, 105. Sotheby Parke Bernet, London title page, pp. 60, 93, 108, 127. Spode-Copeland Museum p. 32. Mrs M. Stephens p. 39. Victoria and Albert Museum, London pp. 9, 20, 24, 30, 41, 47, 48, 59, 75, 79, 91, 113, 116, 133. Watkin-Garratt collection p. 43.